Solve It!

Problem-Solving Strategies

Principal Authors
Myrna Mitchell
Michelle Pauls

Contributing Authors
Suzy Gazlay
Carol Gossett
Kay Kent

Editors
Michelle Pauls
Betty Cordel

Illustrators
Dawn DonDiego
Broc Heasley
Ben Hernandez
Reneé Mason
Margo Pocock
Dave Schlotterback
Brenda Wood

Desktop Publisher
Roxanne Williams

Proofreader
Barbara Horn

This book contains materials developed by the AIMS Education Foundation. **AIMS** (**A**ctivities **I**ntegrating **M**athematics and **S**cience) began in 1981 with a grant from the National Science Foundation. The non-profit AIMS Education Foundation publishes hands-on instructional materials (books and the quarterly magazine) that integrate curricular disciplines such as mathematics, science, language arts, and social studies. The Foundation sponsors a national program of professional development through which educators may gain both an understanding of the AIMS philosophy and expertise in teaching by integrated, hands-on methods.

Copyright © 2005 by the AIMS Education Foundation

All rights reserved. No part of this work may be reproduced or transmitted in any form or by any means—graphic, electronic, or mechanical, including photocopying, taping, or information storage/retrieval systems—without written permission of the publisher unless such copying is expressly permitted by federal copyright law. The following are exceptions to the foregoing statements:

- A person or school purchasing this AIMS publication is hereby granted permission to make up to 200 copies of any portion of it, provided these copies will be used for educational purposes and only at that school site.

- An educator providing a professional development workshop is granted permission to make up to 35 copies of student activity sheets or enough to use the lessons one time with one group.

Schools, school districts, and other non-profit educational agencies may purchase duplication rights for one or more books for use at one or more school sites. Contact the AIMS Education Foundation for specific, current information. Address inquiries to Duplication Rights, AIMS Education Foundation, P.O. Box 8120, Fresno, CA 93747-8120, toll-free (888)733-2467.

ISBN: **1-932093-15-X**

Printed in the United States of America

Solve It! 2nd.
Problem-Solving Strategies

Introduction v	*Work Backwards* Introduction 133
Problem-Solving Strategies vi	Counting Back Answers 134
Strategy Reference vii	Turning Back Time 136
	Change Confusion 143
Guess and Check Introduction 1	Trip Trackers 154
Suitcase Solutions 2	
Adding Up Arrays 11	*Wish for an Easier Problem* Introduction ... 158
Shaping Up Symmetry 21	Tile Tallies 159
	Alphabet Soup 161
Look for Patterns Introduction 30	Two-Colored Trains 164
Domino Designs 31	
Puzzling Patterns 37	Practice Problems 171
Pondering Patterns 42	

Use Manipulatives Introduction 48
Fishy Fractions 49
Card Combos 54
Sweet Squares 57

Draw out the Problem Introduction 63
Counting Clues 64
A-counting for Apples 69
Picturing a Solution 72

Write a Number Sentence Introduction 73
Telling Tales 74
Frog Tales 84
Equation Creation 89

Use Logical Thinking Introduction 94
Seasonal Logic 95
Arranging Astronauts 106
Teddy Bears on a Toboggan 114

Organize the Information Introduction ... 118
Fishy Findings 119
Playing with Probability 124
Sign-in Sheets and Data Displays 129

Introduction

Solve It! 2nd: Problem-Solving Strategies is a collection of activities designed to introduce young children to nine problem-solving strategies. The tasks included will engage students in active, hands-on investigations that allow them to apply their number, measurement, computation, geometry, data organization, and algebra skills in problem-solving settings.

It can be difficult for teachers to shift from teaching math facts and procedures to teaching with an emphasis on mathematical processes and thinking skills. One might ask why problem solving should be taught at all. The most obvious reason is that it is part of most mathematics curricula. However, it is also an interesting and enjoyable way to learn mathematics; it encourages collaborative learning, and it is a great way for students to practice mathematical skills. This in turn leads to better conceptual understanding—an understanding that allows students to remember skills and be able to apply them in different contexts.

Introducing students to the nine strategies included in this book gives them a toolbox of problem-solving methods that they can draw from when approaching problems. Different students might approach the same problem in a variety of ways, some more sophisticated than others. Hopefully, every child can find one approach that he or she can use to solve the problems that you present. Over time, and from discussing what other children have done, students will develop and extend the range of strategies at their disposal.

It is our hope that you will use the problems in this book to enrich your classroom environment by allowing your students to truly experience problem solving. This means resisting the urge to give answers; allowing your students to struggle, and even be frustrated; focusing on the process rather than the product; and providing multiple, repeated opportunities to practice different strategies. Doing this can develop a classroom full of confident problem solvers well equipped to solve problems, both in and out of mathematics for years to come.

Problem-Solving Strategies

 **Guess and Check**

 **Look for Patterns**

 **Use Manipulatives**

 **Draw out the Problem**

 **Write a Number Sentence**

 **Use Logical Thinking**

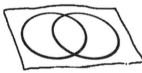 **Organize the Information**

 **Work Backwards**

 **Wish for an Easier Problem**

Activities	Guess and Check	Look for Patterns	Use Manipulatives	Draw out the Problem	Write a Number Sentence	Use Logical Thinking	Organize the Information	Work Backwards	Wish for an Easier Problem
Suitcase Solutions	X		X						
Adding Up Arrays	X	X	X						
Shaping Up Symmetry	X		X						
Domino Designs		X	X						
Puzzling Patterns		X							
Pondering Patterns		X	X			X			
Fishy Fractions			X						
Card Combos			X						
Sweet Squares			X						
Counting Clues				X					
A-counting for Apples			X	X		X			
Picturing a Solution				X					
Telling Tales					X				
Frog Tales			X		X				
Equation Creation		X	X		X			X	
Seasonal Logic			X			X			
Arranging Astronauts			X			X	X		
Teddy Bears on a Toboggan			X			X			
Fishy Findings			X				X		
Playing with Probability			X				X		
Sign-in Sheets and Data Displays							X		
Counting Back Answers			X					X	
Turning Back Time			X					X	
Change Confusion			X					X	
Trip Trackers				X				X	
Tile Tallies			X				X		X
Alphabet Soup			X				X		X
Two-Colored Trains		X	X						X

Problem-Solving Strategies
Guess and Check

The guess and check strategy is helpful when a problem is complicated, has large numbers or a lot of data, or when the problem requires finding one of many possible solutions. This strategy involves guessing the answer, testing to see if it is correct, and using what you have learned to make another guess if the first one is not correct. As students guess and eliminate options, they get closer to the correct answer.

Suitcase Solutions

Topic
Geometry: composing shapes

Key Question
What are the different ways you can pack your tangram pieces into the various suitcases?

Learning Goals
Students will:
1. discover multiple solutions to the packing problem,
2. develop problem-solving and spatial visualization skills, and
3. make accurate records of their solutions.

Guiding Document
NCTM Standards, 2000*
- *Investigate and predict the results of putting together and taking apart two- and three-dimensional shapes*
- *Recognize and apply slides, flips, and turns*
- *Create mental images of geometric shapes using spatial memory and spatial visualization*
- *Recognize and represent shapes from different perspectives*
- *Build new mathematical knowledge through problem solving*

Math
Geometry
  2-D shapes
   combining shapes
Spatial visualization
Problem solving

Integrated Processes
Observing
Comparing and contrasting
Communicating
Recording

Problem-Solving Strategies
Guess and check
Use manipulatives

Materials
Grandfather Tang's Story (see *Curriculum Correlation*)
Two tangram puzzles per student
Large supply of tangram pieces (see *Management 3*)
Glue sticks
Bulletin board space
Student pages

Background Information
This activity makes use of the popular tangram puzzle in a new way. The tangram is an ancient puzzle that has been traced to China, although no one knows how long ago it was actually created. Popular tradition says that the tangram shapes were first "discovered" when a man dropped a square tile and it broke into seven pieces. He spent a long time trying to return the pieces to their original square shape. Since then the tangram puzzle has become popular all over the world. Some historical figures who were fascinated with it include Lewis Carroll (the Oxford mathematician Charles Dodgson), Sam Loyd (the noted American puzzle creator), and Theodore Roosevelt.

In this activity, students are asked to pack four different "suitcases" using two sets of tangram pieces so that the space in each is filled completely. They are challenged to find as many different ways to do this as they can. It is important to emphasize that the suitcases must be filled completely, and that the tangram pieces may not overlap in any way. The suitcases that students will "pack" come in four shapes: a square, a triangle, a parallelogram, and a rectangle. Each of these suitcases has multiple possible solutions that use different numbers and combinations of pieces. As mentioned, students will have two sets of tangram pieces with which to work, reducing the difficulty of the problem and increasing the number of solutions.

Management
1. In order to do this activity with your class, each student will need two sets of tangram pieces. A page of tangram pieces is provided that you can copy, or you can purchase commercial versions of the puzzle on the Internet or at many toy stores. Another option is to use the Ellison die cut of tangram pieces. If you copy the page provided or use the Ellison machine to cut your puzzles, it is recommended that you laminate the paper or use card stock to make the pieces more durable.
2. All of the student pages are designed to be used with pieces the size of those cut from an Ellison die. If you use a different-sized puzzle, you will need to adjust the size of the suitcases on the student pages. (This tangrams on the page provided to copy are the same size as the Ellison die pieces.)

3. In order for students to record their solutions, cut out a large supply of tangram pieces from colored paper using the Ellison machine. Once students discover a solution using their puzzle sets, they can find the corresponding pieces from the supply of puzzle pieces and use a glue stick to paste them to the solution papers provided. These papers can be posted on a bulletin board to create a class solution display. Students can compare and contrast the various solutions for each suitcase, and try to identify those solutions that are unique and those that are merely flips and/or rotations of other solutions.
4. This activity can be spread out over the course of several days to a week to allow students to discover many different solutions for each suitcase.

Procedure
1. To set the stage for this lesson, read the book, *Grandfather Tang's Story* by Ann Tompert. Discuss all the ways Grandfather Tang tries to put the pieces back together in the different shapes. Discuss how he was trying to solve a problem and that he found many different solutions.
2. Tell the students they are going to try to solve a different problem using the same pieces used in the story. Tell them that they will be packing suitcases for a trip to Shape Land. Explain that they can only take certain shapes on their trip and that they must pack the suitcases using these shapes. Discuss how some shapes will fit together in their suitcases, and others will not.
3. Give each student two sets of tangram pieces and a copy of the first two student pages.
4. Distribute the recording pages (cut into individual suitcases), glue sticks, and extra tangram pieces, and explain to students how they are to record the solutions they discover by pasting the pieces onto the solution suitcases.
5. Have students "pack" the four suitcases, discovering and recording as many different solutions as they can.
6. Once students have discovered and recorded several solutions for each suitcase, challenge them to only record solutions that are different from the others that have already been discovered. They will have to carefully examine the placement of the pieces used to determine if their solutions are truly unique, or merely flips and/or rotations of previously discovered solutions.
7. Close this activity with a time of class discussion where students can share their solutions and the things they learned from this activity.

Connecting Learning
1. What is the fewest number of pieces you can use to fill the square suitcase? [two] ...the greatest number of pieces? [six]
2. What is the fewest number of pieces you can use to fill the triangle suitcase? [two] ...the greatest number of pieces? [six]
3. What is the fewest number of pieces you can use to fill the parallelogram suitcase? [two] ...the greatest number of pieces? [six]
4. What is the fewest number of pieces you can use to fill the rectangle suitcase? [four] ...the greatest number of pieces? [10]
5. Can you find a solution for each suitcase that uses three pieces? ...four pieces? ...five pieces? ...etc.
6. Could you fill a circular suitcase? [no] Why or why not? [The pieces do not have rounded edges.]

Extensions
1. Discuss the relationships that exist among the shapes. For example, the square, the parallelogram, and the medium triangle can all be made by combining two small triangles in various configurations.
2. Have students write short stories illustrated by tangram arrangements.
3. Have students develop new shapes using their tangram pieces and challenge their classmates to build them.
4. As a class, explore the history and origin of the tangram.

Solutions
The diagrams shown below give a few of the many possible solutions for filling each suitcase. The solutions that show the fewest number of pieces are unique. The solutions that show the greatest number of pieces are each one of many possibilities.

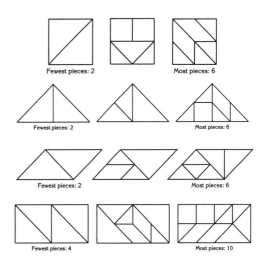

Curriculum Correlation
Tompert, Ann. *Grandfather Tang's Story*. Dragonfly Books. New York. 1997.

* Reprinted with permission from *Principles and Standards for School Mathematics,* 2000 by the National Council of Teachers of Mathematics. All rights reserved.

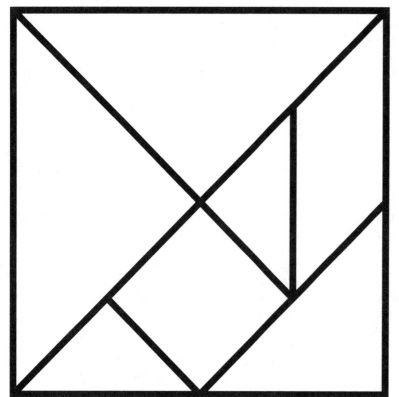

Copy this page onto card stock and laminate for durability. Each student will need two sets of tangram puzzles.

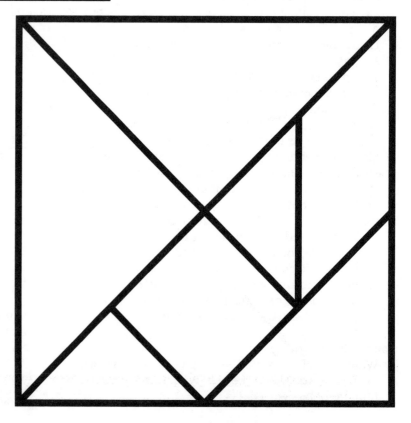

Suitcase Solutions

Fill in the suitcases with tangram pieces.

Find as many ways as you can.

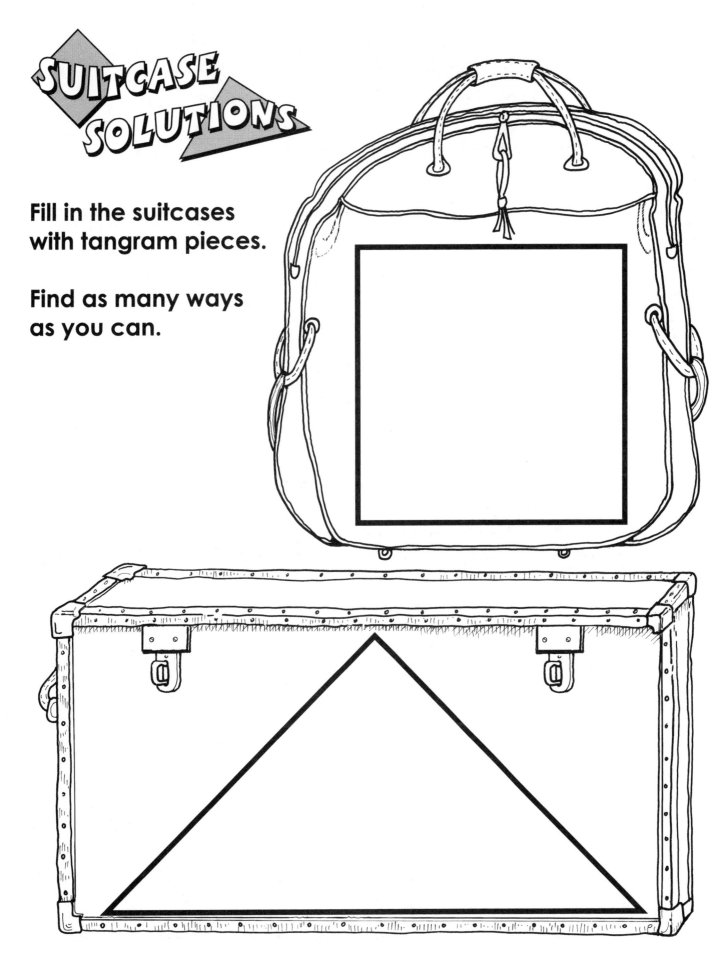

SUITCASE SOLUTIONS

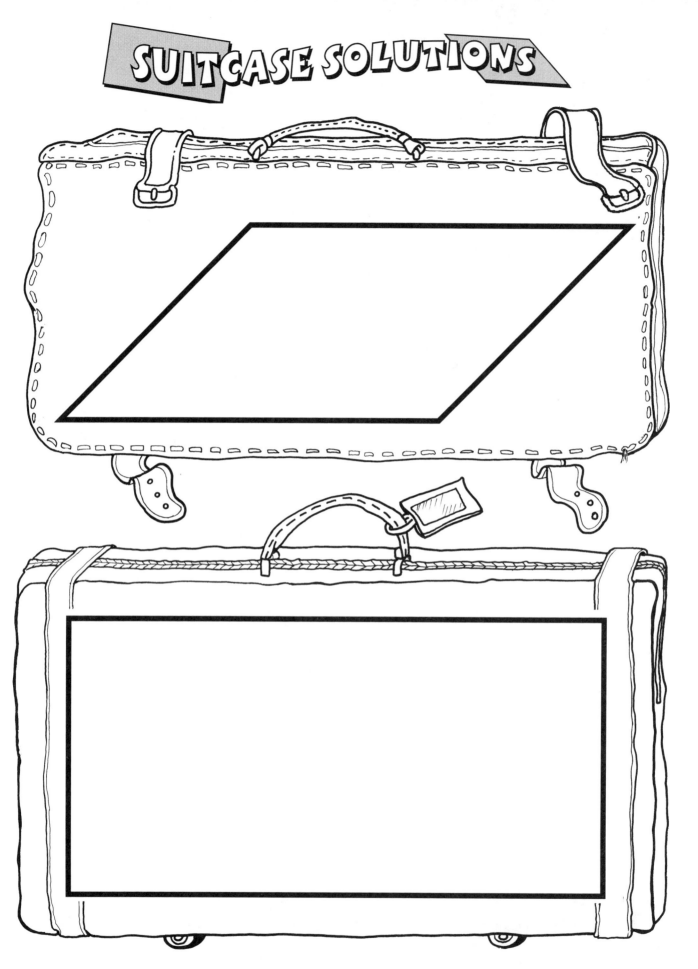

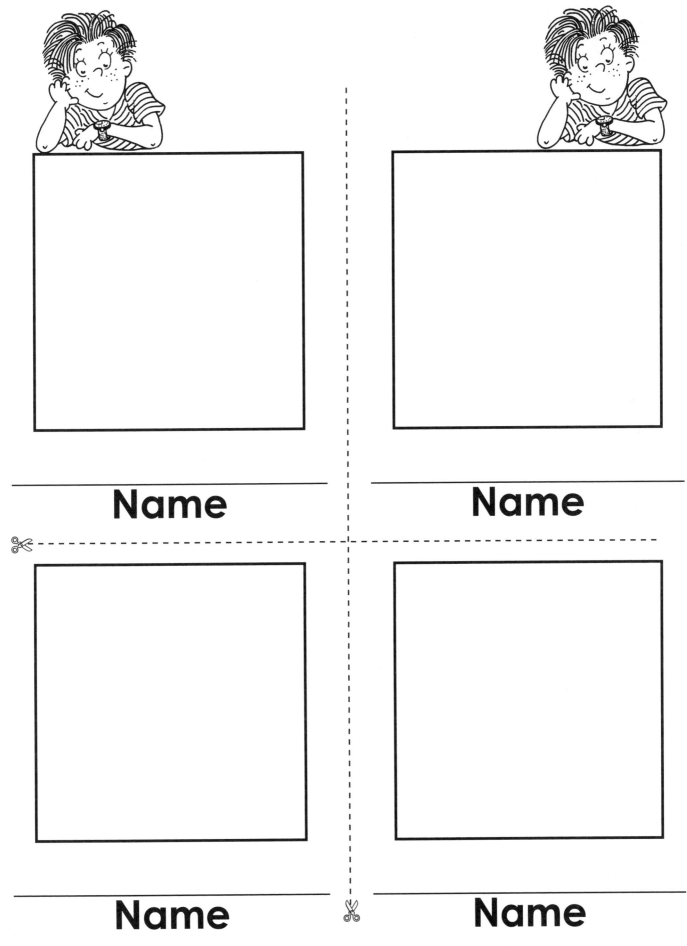

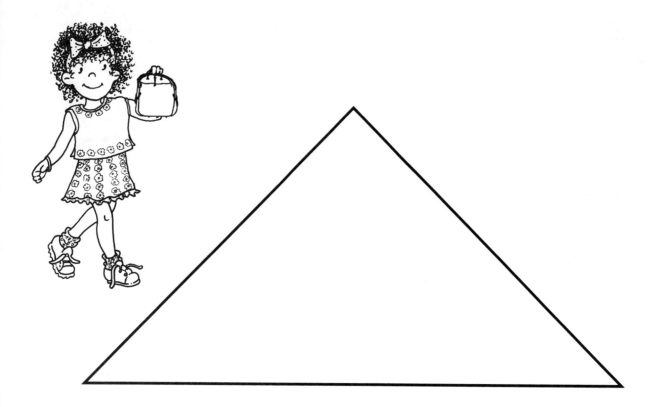

Name:_____

✂ -

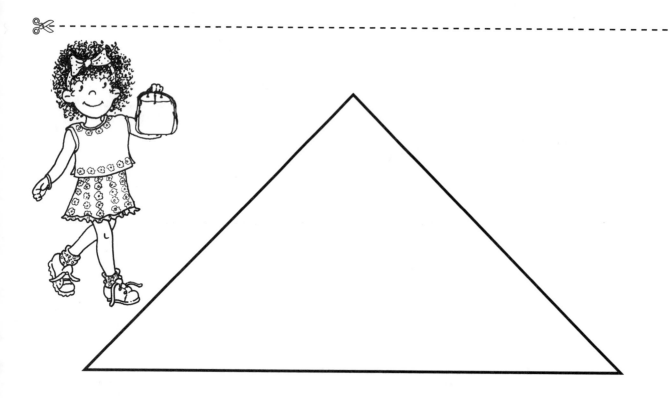

Name:_____

SOLVE IT! 2nd © 2005 AIMS Education Foundation

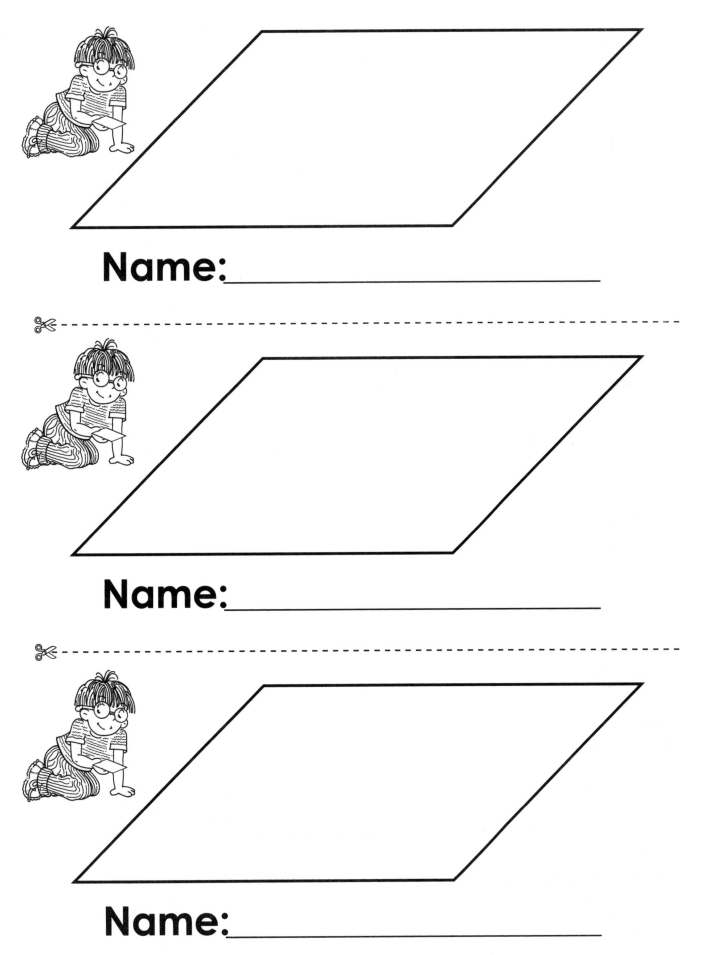

Name:_____

✂----------------------------

Name:_____

✂----------------------------

Name:_____

SOLVE IT! 2ⁿᵈ © 2005 AIMS Education Foundation

Name:_____

✂ -

Name:_____

SOLVE IT! 2nd 10 © 2005 AIMS Education Foundation

Adding Up Arrays

Topic
Problem solving, addition

Key Question
How can you arrange numbers in a variety of arrays so that each line equals a specific target sum?

Learning Goals
The students will:
1. use problem-solving skills to arrange numbers so that they total a target sum,
2. gain practice using addition to solve problems, and
3. look for patterns in their solutions.

Guiding Document
NCTM Standards 2000*
- *Develop fluency with basic number combinations for addition and subtraction*
- *Understand the effects of adding and subtracting whole numbers*
- *Develop and use strategies for whole-number computations, with a focus on addition and subtraction*
- *Build new mathematical knowledge through problem solving*

Math
Number and operations
   addition
Patterns
Problem solving

Integrated Processes
Observing
Comparing and contrasting
Collecting and recording data
Interpreting data

Problem-Solving Strategies
Guess and check
Look for patterns
Use manipulatives

Materials
For each student:
   student pages
   small sticky notes (see *Management 1*)

Background Information
Mathematical microworlds are problems that are governed by simple rules and structures. In this case, a variety of arrays are given and the task is to fill them with the numbers from one to five so that each line has the same sum. At first glance, this activity might appear to be a simple exercise in arithmetic, but if it is used properly, it can open the doors to a rich environment in which students are free to explore, discover, and "do" mathematics.

Each array has multiple solutions, and students will use multiple problem-solving skills as they search for all of the possible answers and give reasons for why all have been discovered. The arrays also have virtually unlimited possibilities for extensions, giving students a rare opportunity to take ownership of a problem and explore things that are interesting to them.

Management
1. Students will need number cards labeled with the numerals one to five. These cards should fit into the spaces on the student sheets. Small sticky notes are the right size, or you can cut scratch paper into small rectangles.
2. Four different arrays are provided. The first two have two different target sums each. The second two have three different target sums each.

Procedure
1. Give each student one of the arrays, the corresponding recording page, and a set of number cards.
2. Direct the students to write the appropriate target sum (in pencil) on the line below the array. For the first array, the possible target sums are 6 and 7. For the second array, the possible target sums are 8 and 9. For the third and fourth arrays, the target sums are 8, 9, and 10.
3. Challenge the students to arrange their number cards in the spaces so that the sum of each line in the array equals the target sum given.
4. Once students find a solution, direct them to record it on the appropriate recording page.
5. Challenge the students to find as many different solutions for this target sum as they can. Have them record their solutions and compare them with other classmates.

SOLVE IT! 2ⁿᵈ   © 2005 AIMS Education Foundation

6. Assign a second target sum for the array. Have students find as many solutions as they can for this new sum.
7. Continue by assigning any remaining target sums.
8. Repeat this process with as many of the different arrays as time allows. This time, however, let students determine the target sums.
9. Close with a time of class discussion in which students look for patterns in their solutions and describe what they find.

Connecting Learning
1. What problem-solving strategies did you use to solve the problems?
2. How does your strategy compare to the strategies used by your classmates?
3. Were some problems easier to solve? ...harder to solve? Why?
4. Do any numbers work as target sums? [no] Why or why not? [There are only a few possible sums, depending on the arrangement. Different target sums require different numbers to be placed in the arrays.]
5. Do you think the class has discovered all the possible solutions for each target sum for the different arrays? How can you find out?
6. Look at the solutions on your recording pages. What patterns do you see?
7. What do you think would happen if you used different numbers in the arrays? Why do you think this?

Extensions
1. Use different sets of consecutive numbers to arrive at different target sums. Try the first five odd or even numbers, the first five multiples of three, etc.
2. Allow students to come up with different arrays that use five numbers and trade them with classmates.

* Reprinted with permission from *Principles and Standards for School Mathematics*, 2000 by National Council of Teachers of Mathematics. All rights reserved.

ADDING UP ARRAYS

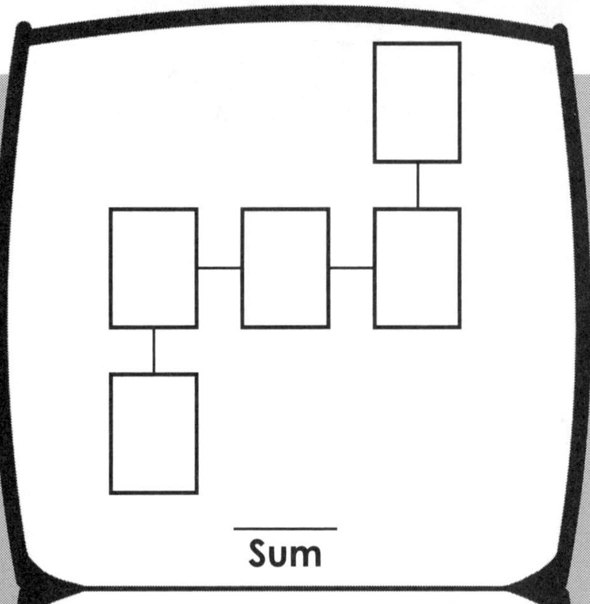

Sum

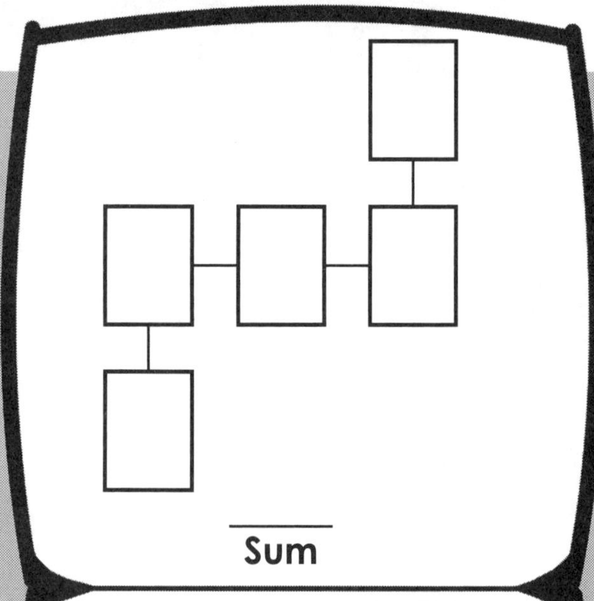

Sum

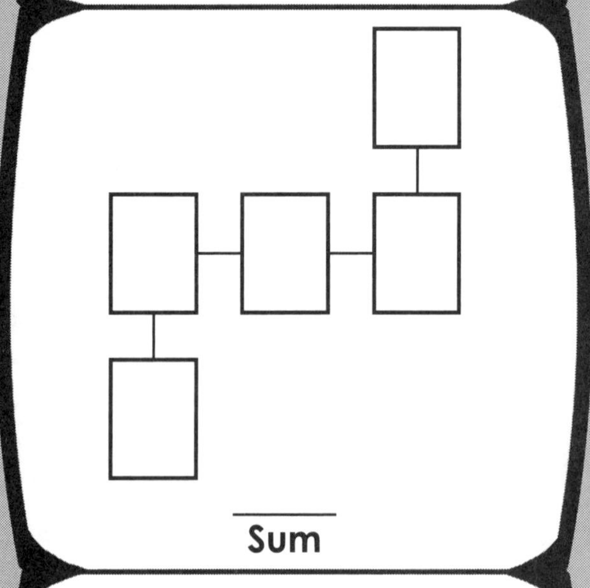

Sum

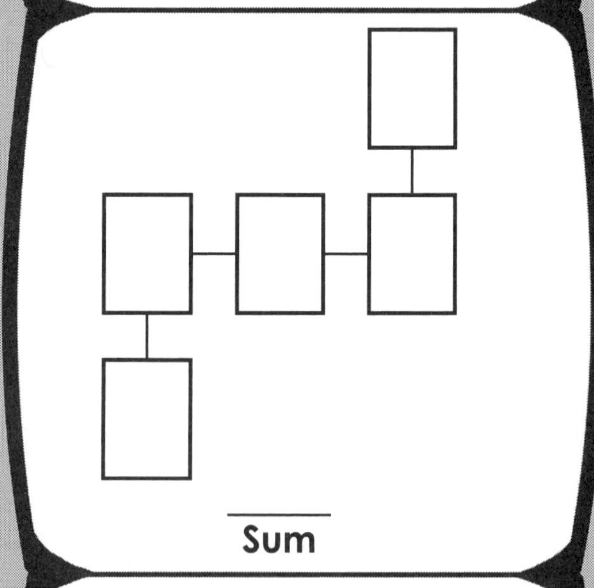

Sum

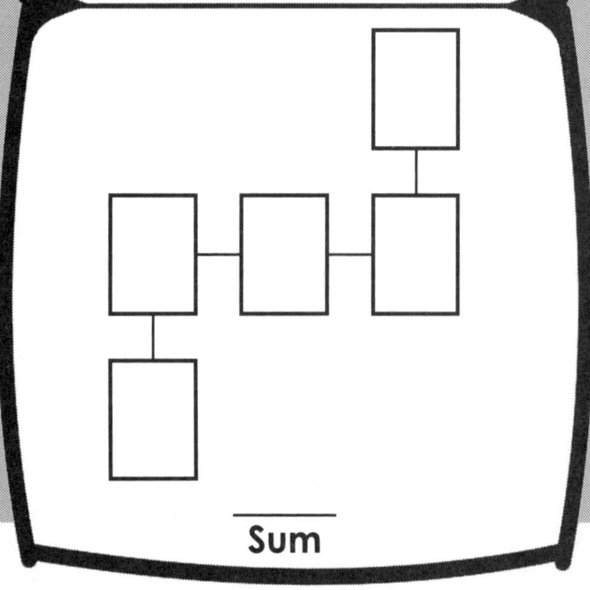

Sum

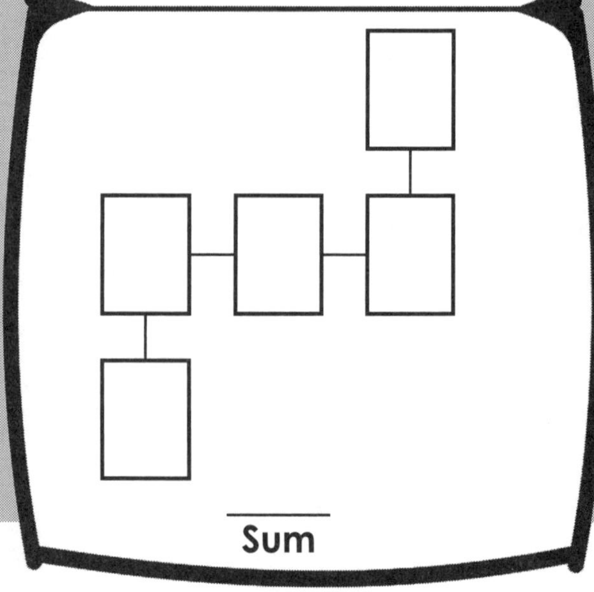

Sum

SOLVE IT! 2nd © 2005 AIMS Education Foundation

Target Sum

ADDING UP ARRAYS

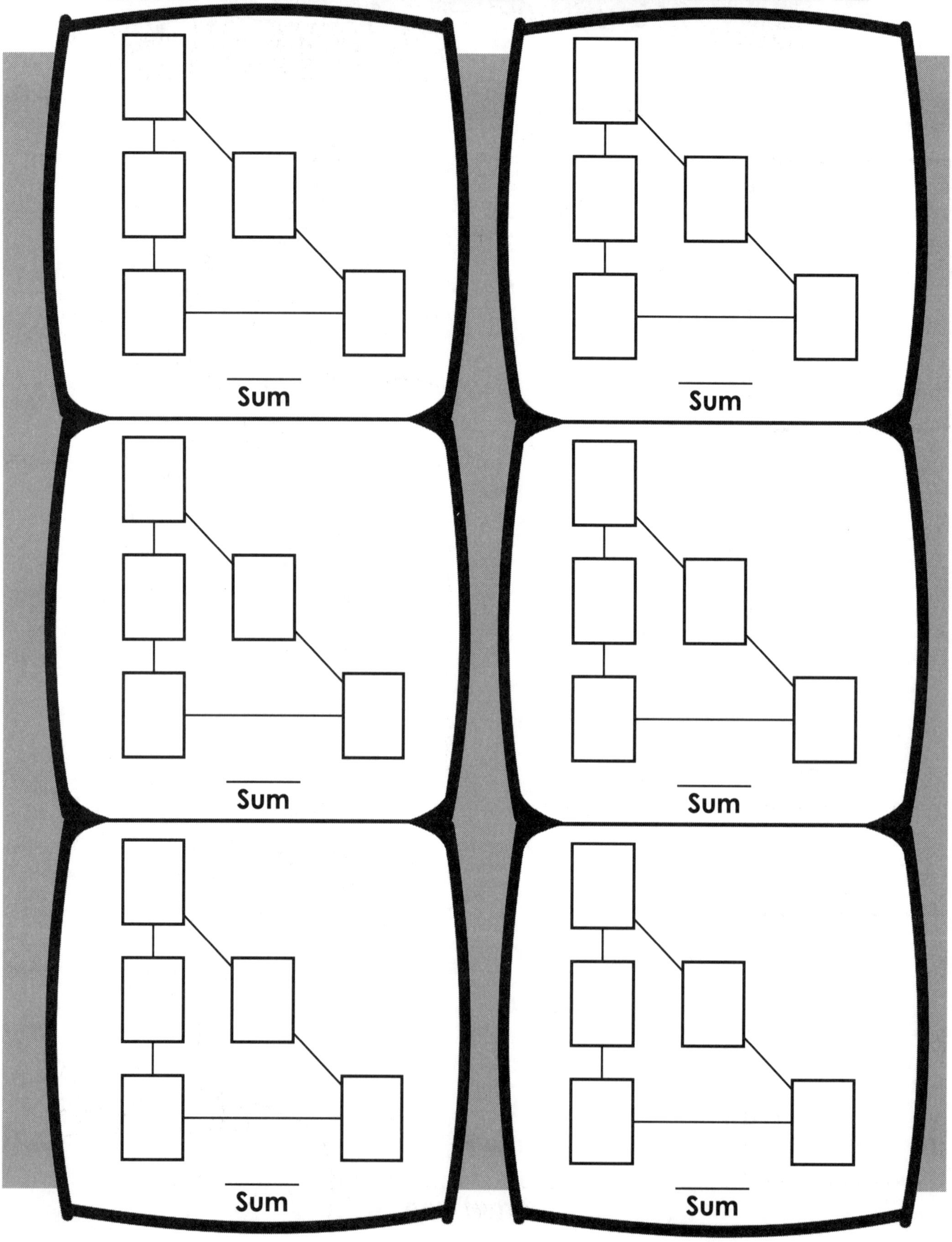

Sum

Sum

Sum

Sum

Sum

Sum

SOLVE IT! 2nd   © 2005 AIMS Education Foundation

ADDING UP ARRAYS

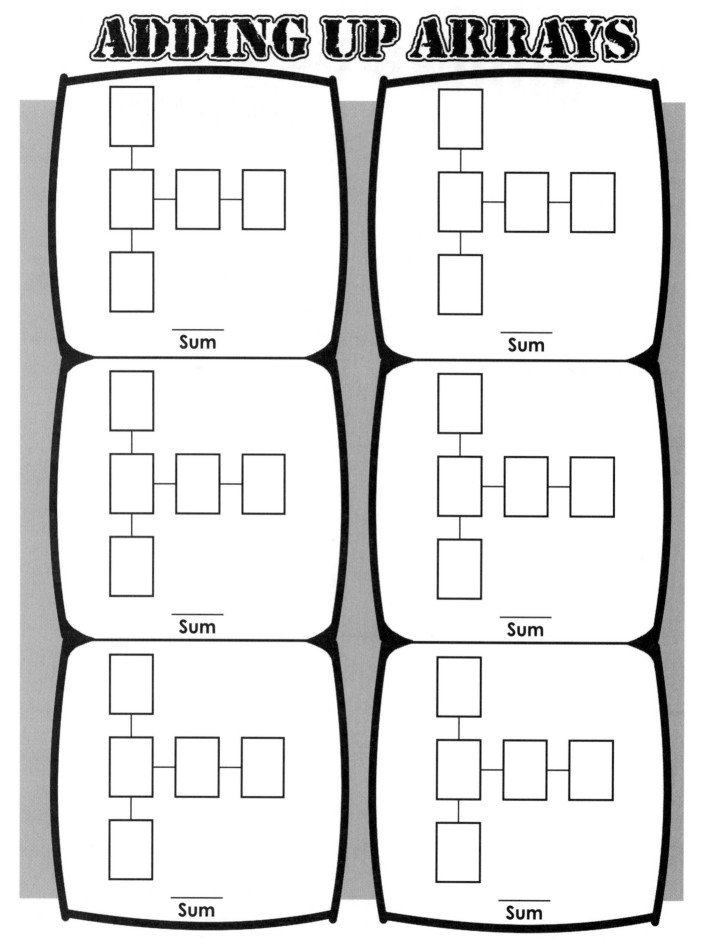

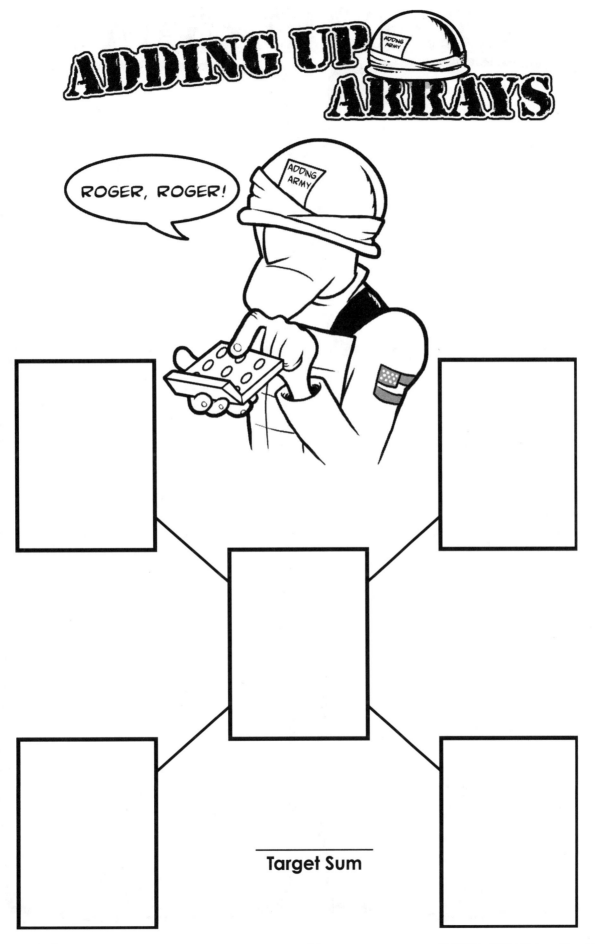

ADDING UP ARRAYS

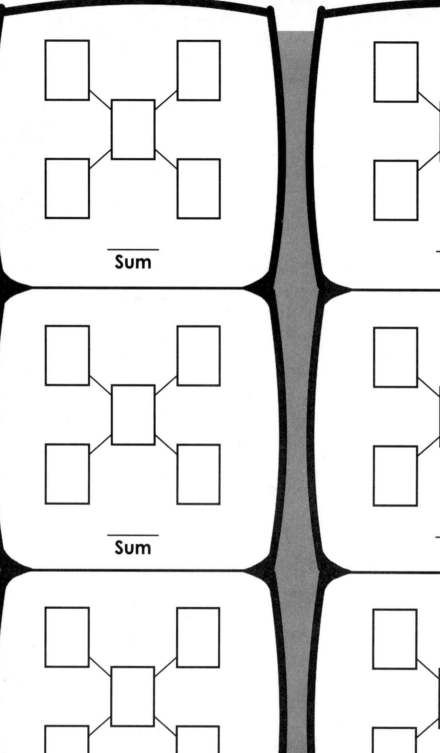

SOLVE IT! 2nd   20   © 2005 AIMS Education Foundation

Shaping Up Symmetry

Topic
Geometry: symmetry

Key Question
How can you fit certain pattern block pieces into a shape so that the pattern they make is symmetrical?

Learning Goals
Students will:
1. fill shapes with pattern block pieces in as many ways as they can,
2. record all of the solutions they can find, and
3. identify the solutions that have lines of symmetry.

Guiding Document
NCTM Standards 2000*
- *Recognize and create shapes that have symmetry*
- *Investigate and predict the results of putting together and taking apart two- and three-dimensional shapes*
- *Build new mathematical knowledge through problem solving*

Math
Geometry
    2-D shapes
    symmetry
Problem solving

Integrated Processes
Observing
Comparing and contrasting
Collecting and recording data
Analyzing

Problem-Solving Strategies
Guess and check
Use manipulatives

Materials
Pattern blocks
Student pages
Colored pencils
Paper pattern block shapes, optional
    (see *Management 4*)
Glue sticks, optional
Mirrors, optional

Background Information
    Pattern blocks are a common manipulative in the primary classroom, and can provide valuable opportunities for students to develop spatial skills and explore concepts of symmetry while simultaneously exercising their problem-solving skills. In this activity, students will use specified pattern blocks to fill large shapes. They will try to find all of the possible ways to do this for one set of shapes, and will identify all of the lines of symmetry in their solutions.

Management
1. Students should work in pairs. Each pair will need a variety of pattern blocks. The shapes needed will depend on the problem assigned.
2. There are three different shape frames for students to fill with pattern blocks, and each frame has three combinations of blocks to be used. Select the shape(s) and combination(s) to be used ahead of time and make the appropriate copies.
3. Make extra copies of the recording pages so that students who discover more than three or four solutions can record everything they find.
4. If you have access to an Ellison die-cut machine, you may want to cut out multiple copies of the pattern block shapes so that students can use these to record their solutions. Instead of tracing around the shapes, they can glue the shapes in the right places on the recording page.
5. This activity is not intended to be an introduction to the concept of symmetry. It is assumed that students are already familiar with line symmetry and are able to identify objects, shapes, patterns, etc., that exhibit line, or mirror, symmetry.

Procedure
1. Review the concept of line symmetry by having students identify the line(s) of symmetry that exist in each of the pattern block shapes.
2. Give each student two hexagon pattern blocks and two blue rhombus pattern blocks. Ask them to put the shapes together in the arrangement shown here.

SOLVE IT! 2nd   21   © 2005 AIMS Education Foundation

3. Ask them to identify the lines of symmetry that exist in this shape. Tell them that they need to look at the colors and the shape. Suggest that they use their pencils to check for lines of symmetry. By laying a pencil across the shape, it is easier to tell if the halves on each side are the same. (If you have mirrors, students can also use these to check for symmetry.)
4. If necessary, repeat this process with a few other simple shapes. Once students are ready to work on the main part of the activity, have them get into pairs and distribute the necessary materials.
5. Go over the instructions, tell them which challenge(s) you would like them to work on, and explain to students how you want them to record their solutions (either by tracing the shapes on the recording page or by gluing down the paper shapes).
6. Allow time for pairs to come up with at least four different solutions for the challenge. (Pairs should have enough pattern blocks so that both can work on the same challenge at the same time.)
7. Have a time of class sharing where students identify how they filled the shapes and the number of lines of symmetry they discovered. Begin with the pair of students who found the most and have them share their solutions with the class.
8. Analyze the solutions to see if there are any that are duplicates (rotations or flips, not unique solutions) or don't have the lines of symmetry claimed.
9. Allow other groups to share any solutions they had that are different from those already shared. As a class, see if you can discover any more solutions that have symmetry.
10. Repeat this activity as desired throughout the year using the other shapes and combinations.

Connecting Learning

1. How do you know if something has a line of symmetry? [both halves are exactly the same]
2. What lines of symmetry are there in the pattern block arrangement you made with two hexagons and two rhombuses?

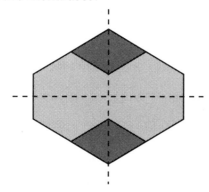

3. How many solutions were you and your partner able to find?
4. Do you think you have found all of the possible solutions? Why or why not?
5. How many lines of symmetry are there in your solutions?
6. How do you know you have found all of the lines of symmetry?
7. Use four pattern blocks to make a shape that has symmetry. Describe the lines of symmetry it has.

Extensions

1. Allow students to fill the frames with any combination of pattern blocks to find patterns with the most lines of symmetry.
2. Challenge students to create a shape that uses at least six pattern blocks and has exactly one line of symmetry ...exactly two lines of symmetry ...three lines of symmetry, etc.
3. Explore rotation symmetry.

Solutions

For each frame two or three solutions have been shown that each exhibit different lines of symmetry. These are only a small sample of the many possible solutions your students should discover.

Small Hexagon Frame
Challenge One

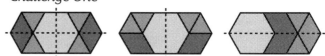

1 hexagon, 2 blue rhombuses, 4 triangles

Challenge Two

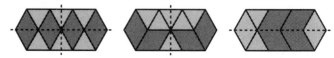

4 blue rhombuses, 6 triangles

Challenge Three

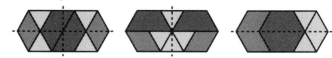

2 trapezoids, 2 blue rhombuses, 4 triangles

Triangle Frame
Challenge One

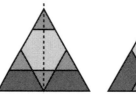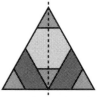

1 hexagon, 4 triangles, 2 trapezoids

Challenge Two

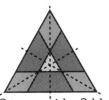 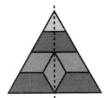

3 trapezoids, 3 blue rhombuses, 1 triangle

Challenge Three

1 hexagon, 1 trapezoid, 2 blue rhombuses, 3 triangles

Large Hexagon Frame
Challenge One

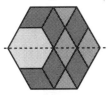 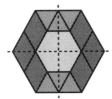 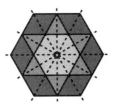

1 hexagon, 6 blue rhombuses, 6 triangles

Challenge Two

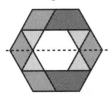 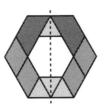 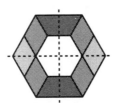

1 hexagon, 2 trapezoids, 4 triangles, 4 blue rhombuses

Challenge Three

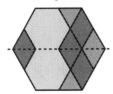 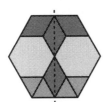 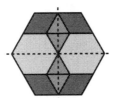

2 hexagons, 4 triangles, 4 blue rhombuses

* Reprinted with permission from *Principles and Standards for School Mathematics*, 2000 by the National Council of Teachers of Mathematics. All rights reserved.

Shaping-Up Symmetry

- Fill the frame with pattern blocks.
- Record each solution you find.
- Count the lines of symmetry in your solutions.
- The group with the most lines of symmetry wins!

❶ Challenge One
Use these shapes:
1 hexagon
2 blue rhombuses
4 triangles

❷ Challenge Two
Use these shapes:
4 blue rhombuses
6 triangles

❸ Challenge Three
Use these shapes:
2 blue rhombuses
2 trapezoids
4 triangles

Shaping-Up Symmetry

- Fill the frame with pattern blocks.
- Record each solution you find.
- Count the lines of symmetry in your solutions.
- The group with the most lines of symmetry wins!

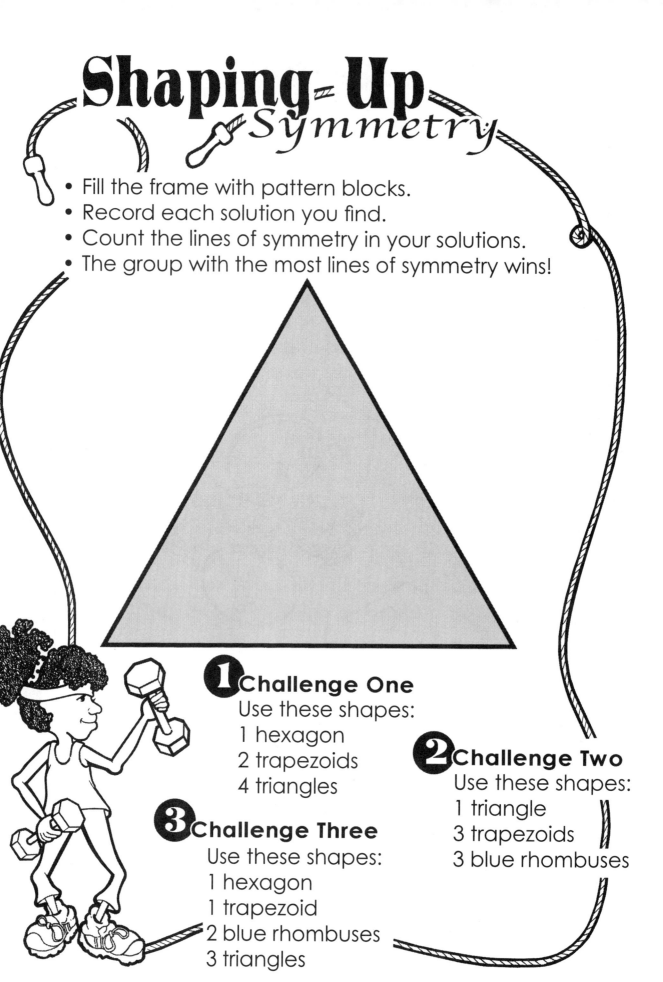

❶ Challenge One
Use these shapes:
1 hexagon
2 trapezoids
4 triangles

❷ Challenge Two
Use these shapes:
1 triangle
3 trapezoids
3 blue rhombuses

❸ Challenge Three
Use these shapes:
1 hexagon
1 trapezoid
2 blue rhombuses
3 triangles

Shaping-Up Symmetry

Record your solutions.
Count the lines of symmetry.

Challenge: _____

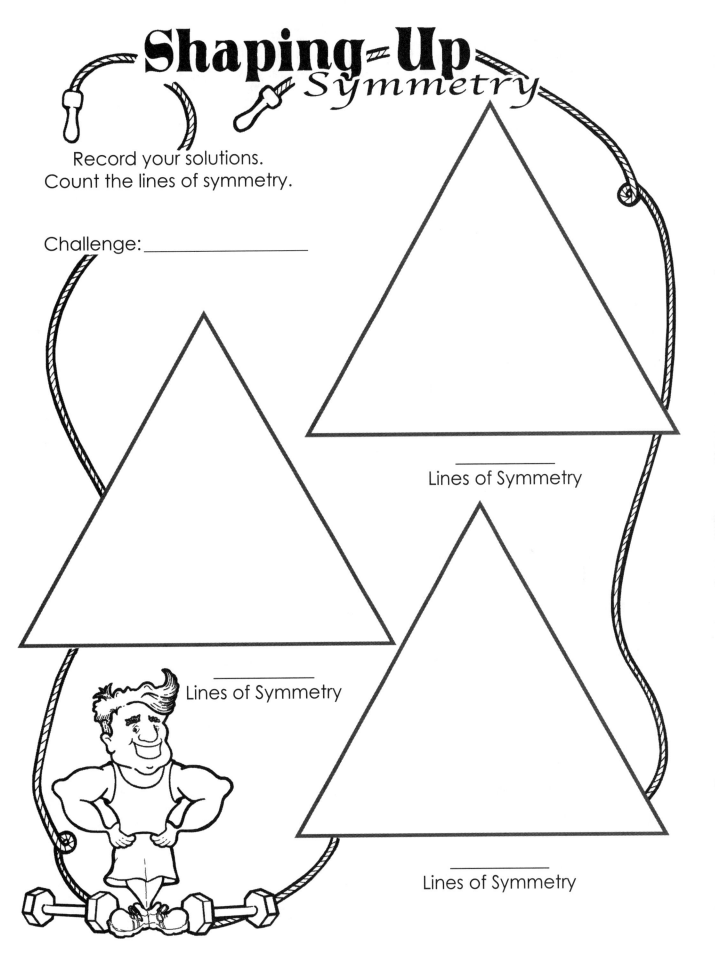

_____
Lines of Symmetry

_____
Lines of Symmetry

_____
Lines of Symmetry

Shaping-Up Symmetry

- Fill the frame with pattern blocks.
- Record each solution you find.
- Count the lines of symmetry in your solutions.
- The group with the most lines of symmetry wins!

❶ Challenge One
Use these shapes:
1 hexagon
6 blue rhombuses
6 triangles

❷ Challenge Two
Use these shapes:
1 hexagon
2 trapezoids
4 triangles
4 blue rhombuses

❸ Challenge Three
Use these shapes:
2 hexagons
4 triangles
4 blue rhombuses

SOLVE IT! 2nd © 2005 AIMS Education Foundation

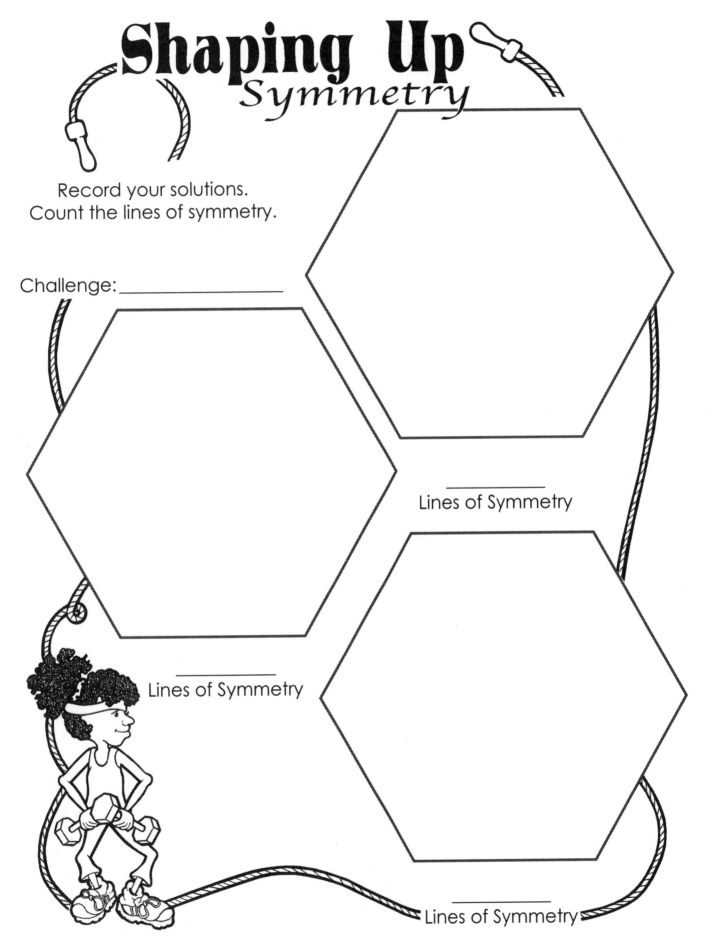

Shaping Up Symmetry

Record your solutions.
Count the lines of symmetry.

Challenge: _____

_____ Lines of Symmetry

_____ Lines of Symmetry

_____ Lines of Symmetry

SOLVE IT! 2nd © 2005 AIMS Education Foundation

Patterns are pervasive in our world. At an early age, children begin to recognize and identify patterns all around them. Looking for patterns is a problem-solving strategy that involves examining relationships between objects, pictures, and numbers. Mathematical problems can often be solved by identifying, extending, and creating patterns.

Domino Designs

Topic
Patterns

Key Questions
1. What patterns can you create using dominoes?
2. What dominoes are missing from the pattern?

Learning Goals
Students will:
1. identify and extend patterns made using dominoes,
2. create their own patterns using dominoes, and
3. find the missing parts to patterns made using dominoes.

Guiding Document
NCTM Standards 2000*
- *Recognize, describe, and extend patterns such as sequences of sounds and shapes or simple numeric patterns and translate from one representation to another*
- *Analyze how both repeating and growing patterns are generated*
- *Build new mathematical knowledge through problem solving*

Math
Patterns
Problem solving

Integrated Processes
Observing
Comparing and contrasting
Recording
Generalizing
Applying

Problem-Solving Strategies
Look for patterns
Use manipulatives

Materials
Dominoes (see *Management 3*)
Transparency of domino tiles
Student pages

Background Information
This activity uses a standard set of double-six dominoes to give students experience creating, extending, and recognizing patterns. Ample opportunities are provided for both creating and recognizing/extending patterns using dominoes. Both growing and repeating patterns can easily be created, and students will benefit from seeing the wide variety of possibilities generated by their classmates. The use of a manipulative that provides a specific set of options helps to keep the problem manageable for young children while still allowing for flexibility in pattern creation.

Management
1. This activity has two parts, and it is intended that students work on it over an extended period of time—at least one to two weeks.
2. If you use centers in your classroom, it may work well to introduce *Part One* of this activity at the beginning of a week and then have it at a center for students to work on for short periods of time each day. At the end of one or two weeks, students can share their discoveries and solutions with the rest of the class and discuss what they learned from the problem.
3. Each student needs his or her own set of dominoes to use while working on this problem. If real sets of dominoes are not available, make a set of dominoes for each student by copying and laminating the page of domino tiles provided. It is a good idea to copy the sets onto different colors of card stock so that it is easy for students to distinguish one set from another.
4. The first student page gives room for students to record their patterns using words and/or pictures. Depending on the number of patterns you want students to record, they may need more than one copy of this page.
5. Make a set of dominoes on transparency film to use on the overhead when introducing each section.

Procedure
Part One
1. Using six of the dominoes copied onto transparency film, make a pattern on the overhead projector. Ask students to identify the pattern.
2. Have a volunteer come to the front and extend the pattern using one of the unused dominoes. Repeat this several times with different kinds of patterns.
3. Tell students that they are going to have the chance to create some patterns of their own using dominoes.
4. Distribute the first student page and a set of dominoes to each student. Give students time to create and record patterns using the dominoes. You may wish to set a quota of one or two patterns to be recorded each time they visit the center or work on the problem.

SOLVE IT! 2ⁿᵈ © 2005 AIMS Education Foundation

5. Encourage students to create as many different patterns as they can using the dominoes and not to be limited to patterns that use the dots. Some of the patterns may simply be the way that the tiles are arranged. A page has been included that gives examples of some of the many patterns that can be made using dominoes.
6. If desired, after students have had several days to explore, establish pattern requirements, such as having a pattern only in the bottom numbers or only in the top numbers, using skip counting as the basis for each pattern, having only even or odd numbers, making patterns using the sums of the numbers on the dominoes, or making patterns that don't use the numbers at all.
7. Have a time of discussion where students can share the patterns they discovered and talk about the processes they went through to generate the different patterns.

Part Two
1. On the overhead, use five dominoes to create a pattern that is missing one tile from the middle. Invite someone to come up and complete the pattern using one of the unused dominoes.
2. Repeat this process several times until students are comfortable filling in the missing domino in the pattern.
3. Have students get into pairs and distribute a set of dominoes and the final student page to each student.
4. Go over the instructions as a class and be sure that everyone understands the challenge.
5. Give the students time to find the missing domino and create patterns of their own to trade with their partners. When doing this section, both students should create a pattern at the same time (either by using one they created in the first section or by thinking of a new one), and then trade so that they each have something to do the whole time. The first challenge is to complete the pattern when one domino has been removed; the second challenge is to complete the pattern with two missing dominoes.
6. Close with a final time of class discussion and sharing.

Connecting Learning
1. How did you identify the patterns that were up on the overhead projector?
2. What kinds of patterns did you create using your dominoes?
3. How are these patterns like the ones your classmates created? How are they different?
4. Name some of the kinds of patterns that can be made with a set of dominoes.
5. Was it harder to extend the patterns or to find the missing pieces to the patterns? Why?
6. Was your partner able to fill in the domino(es) missing from your pattern? Why or why not?
7. Were you able to fill in the domino(es) missing from your partner's pattern? Why or why not?
8. What did you learn about patterns from this activity?

Extensions
1. Create a class list of patterns to display in the classroom. An easy way to do this is to make copies of the page of dominoes and have students cut out the dominoes they need for each pattern. These can then be glued to strips of adding machine tape or sentence strips for easy display. For more advanced students, these patterns can be grouped by the rules that govern them.
2. Use sets of double-nine or double-twelve dominoes to create patterns.

* Reprinted with permission from *Principles and Standards for School Mathematics*, 2000 by the National Council of Teachers of Mathematics. All rights reserved.

Sample Domino Patterns

Following are a few examples of the many, many patterns your students may create using their dominoes. Remember not to limit students to patterns that use the numbers. Some patterns may have to do with the physical arrangement of the tiles, or only one row of numbers. Encourage the creative exploration of different possibilities.

This pattern is simply the way the tiles are arranged—one up, one sideways, one up, one sideways, etc.

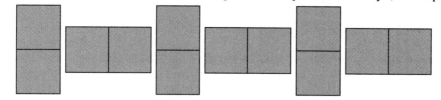

Another pattern might be one tile face down, one tile face up, etc. with no attention paid to the numbers on the tiles.

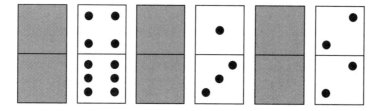

Here the pattern is the consecutive doubles starting with double ones and going to double sixes.

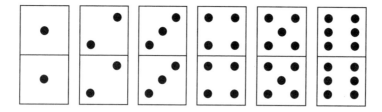

This pattern alternates blanks with doubles, increasing from one to three.

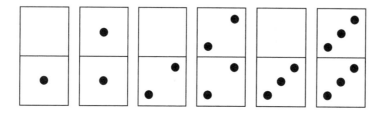

Here the pattern is in the sums of the tiles. The first tile has a sum of three, the second has a sum of four, the third has a sum of five, and so on.

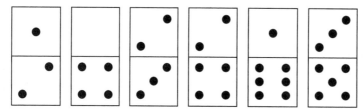

SOLVE IT! 2nd © 2005 AIMS Education Foundation

Domino Designs
Domino Tiles

Domino Designs

Choose any six dominoes from your set. Make a pattern. Record your pattern.

My Domino Pattern:

Make some new patterns with different dominoes. Record each one. Try to get lots of different patterns.

My Domino Pattern:

My Domino Pattern:

Study the pattern below.

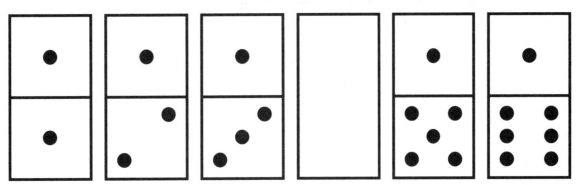

What is missing from this pattern? Find the missing domino in your set. Complete the pattern.

Challenge One:

Make your own patterns in the spaces below. Give it to your partner with one domino missing.

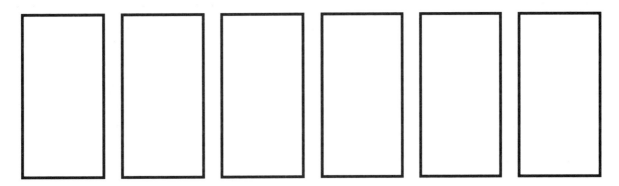

What is missing from this pattern? Find the missing domino. Complete the pattern.

Challenge Two:

Make a different pattern in the same spaces. Take out two dominoes. Give it to your partner to solve.

Topic
Patterns

Key Question
What number patterns can we find on a hundreds chart?

Learning Goals
Students will:
1. identify number patterns on a hundreds chart, and
2. extend the patterns by filling in missing numbers in given sections of the hundreds chart.

Guiding Document
*NCTM Standards 2000**
- *Recognize, describe, and extend patterns such as sequences of sounds and shapes or simple numeric patterns and translate from one representation to another*
- *Build new mathematical knowledge through problem solving*
- *Solve problems that arise in mathematics and in other contexts*

Math
Patterns
Number sense
Problem solving

Integrated Processes
Observing
Comparing and contrasting
Classifying
Predicting

Problem-Solving Strategy
Look for patterns

Materials
Hundreds chart (see *Management 2*)
Puzzle pieces (see *Management 3*)
Crayons
Transparency pens

Background Information
One of the goals for young children is that they develop an understanding of the properties of and relationships among numbers. Since the understanding of patterns contributes to their understanding of number, this activity is focused around the number patterns on a hundreds chart.

This activity provides an opportunity for students to explore and identify the patterns contained in a hundreds chart and to use logical thinking to complete various number patterns.

Management
1. This activity could be used as part of a 100th day of school celebration.
2. Make one copy of the hundreds chart for each student and one transparency for the overhead.
3. A set of puzzle pieces has been provided for you; however, you may choose to create your own by cutting apart a copy of the hundreds chart and erasing numbers from various spaces (use white correction fluid or tape). This allows you to raise or lower the difficulty level. One set of puzzle pieces should be copied on transparency film and cut out for use on the overhead projector. The second set of puzzle pieces should be copied for each student to work on independently.

Procedure
1. Distribute a copy of the hundreds chart to each student. Ask the students to look closely at the chart to see if they can find any number patterns.
2. Place the hundreds chart transparency on the overhead and invite a student to come forward and point out a number pattern they discovered. Color in the pattern on the transparency and instruct the class to do the same on their copies of the hundreds chart. Encourage other students to identify number patterns they see on the chart. Using different colored markers, color in the patterns on the transparency and have the class do likewise.
3. After each child has had an opportunity to identify a pattern on the hundreds chart, ask students if they think that they could fill in a blank hundreds chart on their own. Ask them to recall some of the counting patterns that make up the chart. Tell the students that instead of filling in the entire chart, you have taken the hundreds chart and cut it into puzzle pieces that you would like them to help you complete.
4. Place one of the transparency puzzle pieces with only a few missing numbers on the overhead. Have the class study the piece for a few minutes then ask if they recognize it as part of the hundreds chart. You may choose to talk about where it would

SOLVE IT! 2nd © 2005 AIMS Education Foundation

be found on the chart, (top left side, bottom right part, etc.) When the class can recognize that it is a part of the whole chart, question them about the missing numbers. Invite several students to help you fill in the puzzle piece. Each time students fill in a box, ask them what strategy they used to decide what number belonged in the box.

5. Continue placing puzzle pieces on the overhead, gradually increasing the number of blank boxes each time. When you feel that the students are confident in their ability to complete the number patterns, allow them to try the second set of puzzle pieces on their own.
6. When students have completed their puzzle pieces, discuss the strategies they used and the number patterns involved.

Connecting Learning
1. Tell about one pattern you found on the hundreds chart. How would you describe it to a friend?
2. What strategy did you use to complete the puzzle pieces?
3. What pattern do you see when you begin with two and count by twos?
4. What happens if you skip-count by tens and start with 37? What do you notice?
5. How would adding 10 to any number be like skip-counting by tens?
6. Skip-counting by what numbers will include 100 as part of the pattern?
7. What do you notice when you begin with one and count by twos? Explain?

Extension
Have students create their own puzzle pieces using grid paper.

* Reprinted with permission from *Principles and Standards for School Mathematics*, 2000 by the National Council of Teachers of Mathematics. All rights reserved.

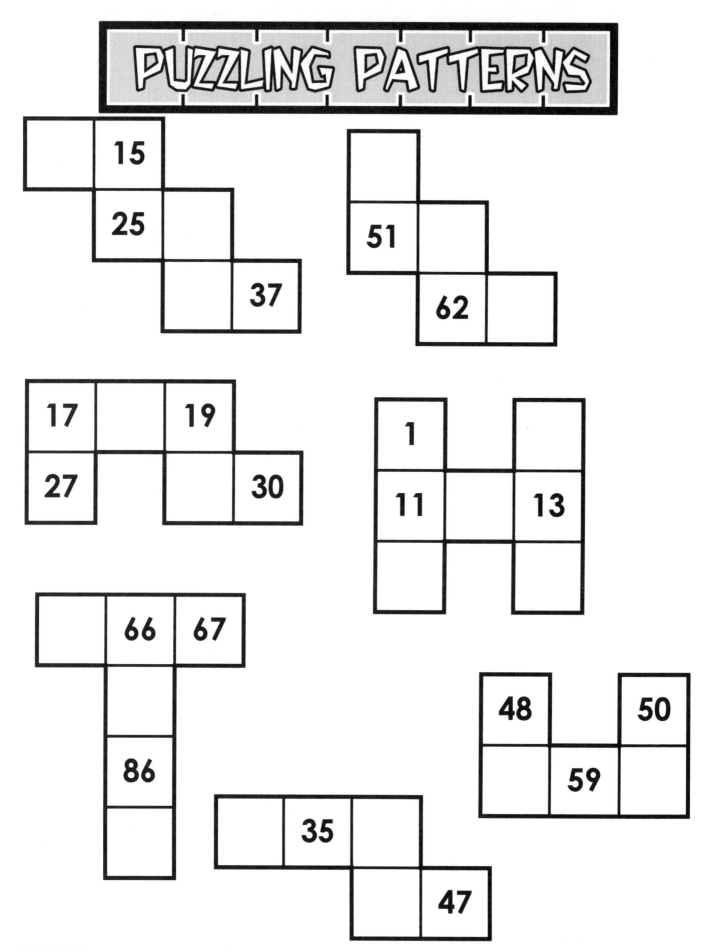

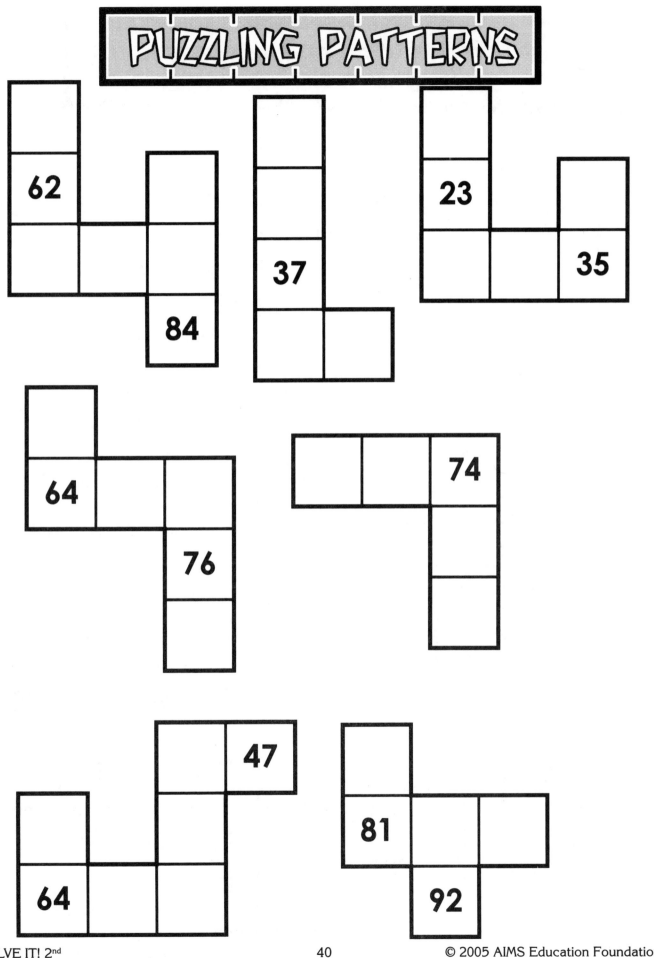

PUZZLING PATTERNS

1	2	3	4	5	6	7	8	9	10
11	12	13	14	15	16	17	18	19	20
21	22	23	24	25	26	27	28	29	30
31	32	33	34	35	36	37	38	39	40
41	42	43	44	45	46	47	48	49	50
51	52	53	54	55	56	57	58	59	60
61	62	63	64	65	66	67	68	69	70
71	72	73	74	75	76	77	78	79	80
81	82	83	84	85	86	87	88	89	90
91	92	93	94	95	96	97	98	99	100

Pondering Patterns

Topic
Patterns

Key Question
What comes next?

Learning Goals
Students will:
1. recognize, describe, complete, extend patterns; and
2. translate patterns from one representation to another.

Guiding Documents
Project 2061 Benchmark
- Patterns can be made by putting different shapes together or taking them apart.

NCTM Standards 2000*
- Recognize, describe, and extend patterns such as sequences of sounds and shapes or simple numeric patterns and translate from one representation to another
- Analyze how both repeating and growing patterns are generated
- Sort, classify, and order objects by size, number, and other properties
- Build new mathematical knowledge through problem solving
- Solve problems that arise in mathematics and in other contexts

Math
Patterns
Measurement
Problem solving

Integrated Processes
Observing
Comparing and contrasting
Classifying
Predicting

Problem-Solving Strategies
Look for patterns
Use manipulatives
Use logical thinking

Materials
Mr. Noisy's Book of Patterns
  (see *Curriculum Correlation*)
Pattern task cards (see *Management 3*)
Pattern holder (see *Management 4*)
Sentence strips (see *Management 5*)
12" x 18" construction paper
Manipulatives (see *Management 6*)
Tool page (see *Management 6*)
Transparencies

Background Information
Looking for patterns is a problem-solving strategy that involves examining the relationship between objects, pictures, or numbers, and predicting what will come next or what will happen over time. This activity provides an opportunity for students to identify, extend, and create different types of patterns, including growing patterns, and to use logical thinking to solve problems.

Management
1. It is expected that the children have had prior experience identifying and extending patterns.
2. Copy several sets of the pattern task cards onto card stock and laminate for extended use.
3. The pattern task cards included in this lesson can be used as station cards, book pages for individual student books, or one at a time as a "bright beginning" to math class.
4. To make the pattern holder used in *Part One* of this activity, place a 12" x 18" piece of construction paper horizontally on the table in front of you. Position a sentence strip about one centimeter from the top of the paper and fold over along the bottom edge of the sentence strip. Remove the sentence strip and continue folding until you reach the edge of the paper. Tape the loose edge down; the side with the tape will be the back of your pattern holder. Next, cut a window out of the front as indicated in the diagram and decorate the cover. Place the window in the left side of the sleeve so that students will read patterns from left to right.

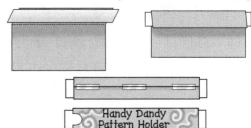

SOLVE IT! 2ⁿᵈ © 2005 AIMS Education Foundation

5. Using sentence strips, create several patterns for the students to identify and extend. Below is a suggested set of pattern strips that include growing patterns, color patterns, positional patterns, and number patterns.

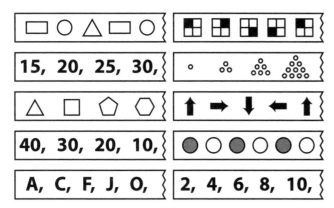

6. To solve each pattern task card, students will need various manipulatives. They can use manipulatives from the classroom such as rulers, meter-tapes, Unifix cubes, area tiles, pattern blocks, etc., or you can copy the tool page included onto card stock for each student or center. The students will need inch rulers to measure the fishing hooks and centimeter rulers to measure the snail trails.
7. Make overhead transparencies of each of the pattern task cards.

Procedure

Part One
1. Read *Mr. Noisy's Book of Patterns* to the class. As each page is read, have the children identify the pattern, discuss how many parts each pattern has, and translate the pattern to letters, objects, etc. For example, when Mr. Noisy laughs, he goes, Hee-Hee-Haw, Hee-Hee-Haw. This is a three-part pattern. In objects it could be pencil, pencil, eraser, pencil, pencil, eraser. In body movements it could be snap, snap, clap, snap, snap, clap; and in letters it could be AABAAB.
2. After discussing the book, display your handy dandy pattern holder containing a pattern strip and challenge your students to identify and extend the pattern. Reveal one part of the pattern and ask the students what might come next in the pattern. Discuss reasonable suggestions, then reveal the second part of the pattern. After each part of the pattern is revealed, say, "I'm beginning to see a pattern, are you?" and ask the students to predict what would logically come next.
3. Repeat *Procedure 2* using additional pattern strips.
4. As students gain an understanding of color and shape patterns, ask them questions that focus on numbers. For example, "What would appear in the sixth position of the pattern? ...ninth position? ...12th position?" Then move on to patterns in numbers such as counting by fives or tens, examine patterns found in two-digit numbers, and help students to identify the odd and even number patterns.
5. When the students have demonstrated their ability to recognize and extend patterns, distribute blank sentence strips to students and encourage them to create their own patterns.
6. Have students place their patterns in the pattern holder and allow them to share their patterns with the class.

Part Two
1. Review the different types of patterns covered in *Part One* of this activity.
2. Use the transparencies suggested in *Management 7* to introduce each individual pattern task card.
3. After introducing the pattern task cards, use them at math centers, or begin each math time with a pattern to ponder.

Connecting Learning
1. What is a pattern?
2. Where do we see patterns?
3. If a plant is two inches tall on Monday, three inches tall on Tuesday, and four inches tall on Wednesday, how tall do you think it will be on Thursday? Why?
4. What color cube comes next in this pattern? Red, blue, yellow, red, blue, _____
5. How did you decide what came next in each of the patterns?
6. What might an ABAB pattern look like using body movements? (e.g., snap, clap, snap, clap, etc.)
7. If the pattern is blue hat, red hat, blue hat, red hat, what color hat is in the sixth position of the pattern? How do you know?
8. What might an ABAB pattern look like on the playground? [bar, space, bar, space, or swing, space, swing, space, etc.]
9. Do you think that there are more two-, three-, or four-part patterns in our classroom? Explain your thinking.

Curriculum Correlation
Williams, Rozanne Lanczak. *Mr. Noisy's Book of Patterns.* Creative Teaching Press. Huntington Beach, CA. 1996.

* Reprinted with permission from *Principles and Standards for School Mathematics,* 2000 by the National Council of Teachers of Mathematics. All rights reserved.

Bunches of Buttons

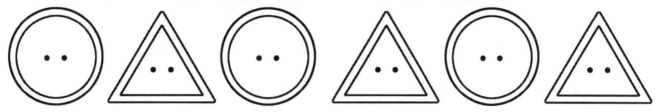

What would this pattern look like in letters?

_____

...in colors?

_____

✂------------------------------

Fishy Features

Which patterns can be made with the fish in the bowl?

1. __   3. __

2. __   4. __

Trying Triangles

What patterns can you make with only s?

Snail Trails

What comes next?

Fishing for Answers
Draw the missing hook.

Bug in a Rug
How many rug patterns can you make with 2 kinds of bugs?

SOLVE IT! 2nd
46
© 2005 AIMS Education Foundation

Tools

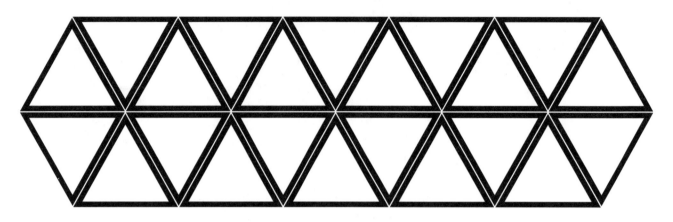

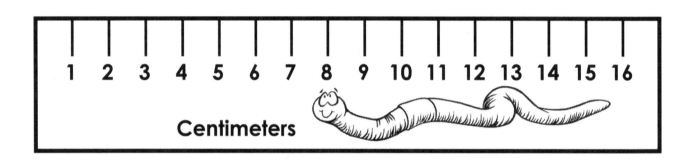

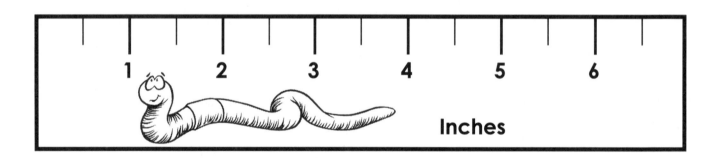

Problem-Solving Strategies
Use Manipulatives

It is often helpful for young children to manipulate objects or act out a problem to arrive at a solution. Using concrete objects to represent the parts of the problem allows them to have all the necessary information in front of them at once. By taking an active role in finding the solution, students are also more likely to remember the process they used and be able to use it again for solving similar problems. This strategy is useful when students need to picture the parts of a problem.

Fishy Fractions

Topic
Fractions

Key Question
How can we use a fishbowl and fish to model fractions?

Learning Goals
Students will:
1. recognize and name fractions as representative of a counted part of a group or set of objects, and
2. use different colored fish to represent fractional parts of a whole set of fish.

Guiding Document
NCTM Standards 2000
- *Understand and represent commonly used fractions, such as $\frac{1}{4}$, $\frac{1}{3}$, and $\frac{1}{2}$*
- *Count with understanding and recognize "how many" in sets of objects*
- *Build new mathematical knowledge through problem solving*
- *Solve problems that arise in mathematics and in other contexts*

Math
Rational numbers
   fractions
Number sense
Counting
Problem solving

Integrated Processes
Observing
Classifying
Comparing and contrasting
Relating

Problem-Solving Strategies
Use manipulatives
Act out the problem

Materials
Overhead transparencies (see *Management 1*)
Multi-colored fish (see *Management 2*)
Student pages (see *Management 3*)
Crayons or colored pencils

Background Information
Many problems we encounter are straightforward and require nothing more than the application of arithmetic rules. However, for young children to truly understand a group or set fraction model, it is important for them to act out a problem or to move objects around while they are trying to solve a problem. They can then see that a group of objects can represent a whole and any part of the group or set can be written as a fraction where the denominator represents the total number in the group or set and the numerator represents the part of the set that shares a common attribute. This allows them to develop visual images of the data in the problem and the solution process. By taking an active role in finding the solution, students are more likely to remember the process they used and be able to use it again for solving similar problems.

In this activity, the children will be using fish as a concrete manipulative and will be taking the problem solving to an abstract level by writing the fractions that represent the dramatizations.

Management
1. Prior to the lesson, copy the fishbowl and student recording page onto overhead transparencies for demonstration purposes.
2. It is suggested that you use multi-colored fish crackers or gummy fish as the manipulative for this activity. However, a page of fish pictures has been provided. If you choose to use the paper fish, the children should color six of the fish purple, six red, six green, six orange, and six yellow.
3. A fishbowl, fish, and student recording page are needed for each student. Have the students record what they acted out on the large fishbowl onto the small fishbowls by drawing the correctly colored fish in each bowl.
4. Remind students to clear their boards after solving each problem.
5. Depending on your students' reading abilities, you may choose to write some of the questions on the board or on sentences strips. This reinforces their reading and is similar to the way they would see problems in a testing situation.
6. Several fraction questions have been provided for you; however, it is suggested that you tailor your own questions so that they will review and reinforce skills that your students are accountable for such as addition, subtraction, and greater-than and less-than concepts.

SOLVE IT! 2nd   © 2005 AIMS Education Foundation

Procedure
1. Give each student a fishbowl, recording page, and fish.
2. Read the following instructions and questions to your students, repeat them, and ask the students to act out the problems using the fishbowl and goldfish. After each problem, discuss what students did on the fishbowl and allow them to make a record by drawing the correct number of colored fish in the small fishbowls on the student-recording page.
   - Place four fish in the bowl. One-half of the fish should be purple and one-half of the fish should be red. How many purple fish are in your bowl? How many red fish are in your bowl?
   - Place two red fish and one green fish in the bowl. What fraction represents the number of green fish in the set? What fraction represents the number of red fish in the set?
   - Place six fish in the bowl. Put two-sixths of the fish in the house and the rest floating in the water. What fraction describes the fish floating in the water?
   - Place two green fish in your fishbowl, one-half of them below the house and one-half above the house. Describe your fishbowl.
   - Place one orange fish on the bottom of the fishbowl, one orange fish in the plants, one orange fish at the top of the water, and one green fish in the house. What fraction of the fish are green? What fraction of the fish are orange?
   - There were five red fish swimming in the fishbowl. One jumped out and landed beside the fishbowl. What fraction of the fish jumped out?
   - Place two yellow fish above the house and two purple fish beside the house. What fraction describes the number of yellow fish in the fishbowl?
   - Place five fish in the bowl. One-fifth of them should be green and the rest should be yellow. How many fish are yellow?
   - Place three fish in the bowl—one in the house and two in the plants. What fraction of the fish are in the plants?
   - Place six fish in a row at the top of the fishbowl. Five-sixths should be purple and one-sixth should be orange. Describe your fishbowl.

Connecting Learning
1. How did working with the fish and fishbowl help you learn more about fractions?
2. How did you know how many fish should be purple if one-half of the set of six were purple?
3. How do you write one-half?
4. Show me one-fourth using fish. What does it look like written as a fraction?
5. What fractions could we use to describe a bowl of fish that has two red fish and one purple fish?
6. How could we represent fractions using students instead of fish?

Extension
Allow students to place fish in the bowl however they want. Have them tell you something about the fish in their bowls using fractions.

* Reprinted with permission from *Principles and Standards for School Mathematics,* 2000 by the National Council of Teachers of Mathematics. All rights reserved.

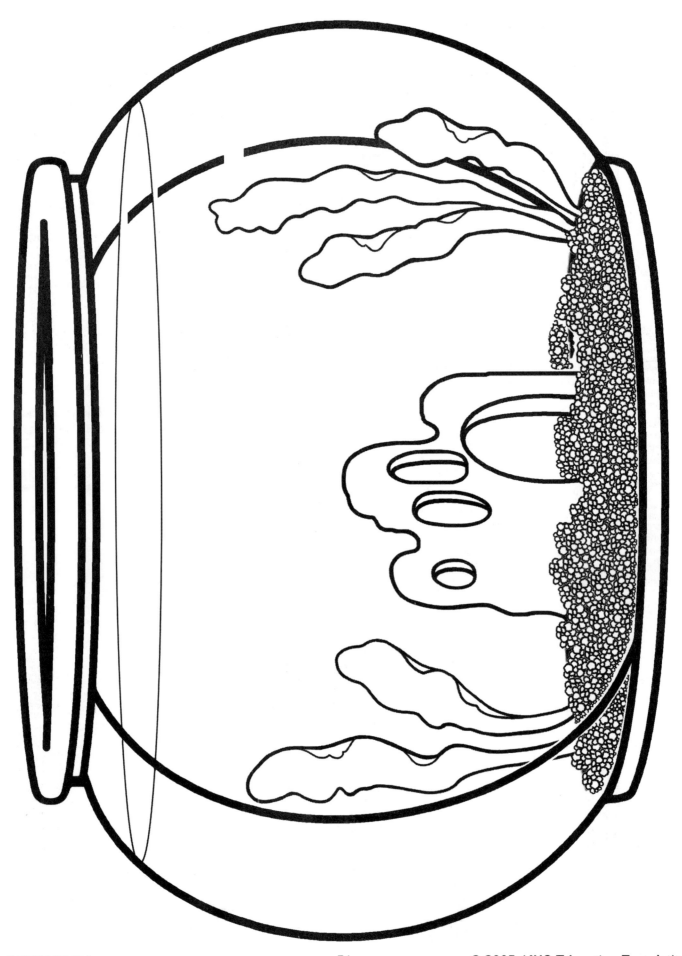

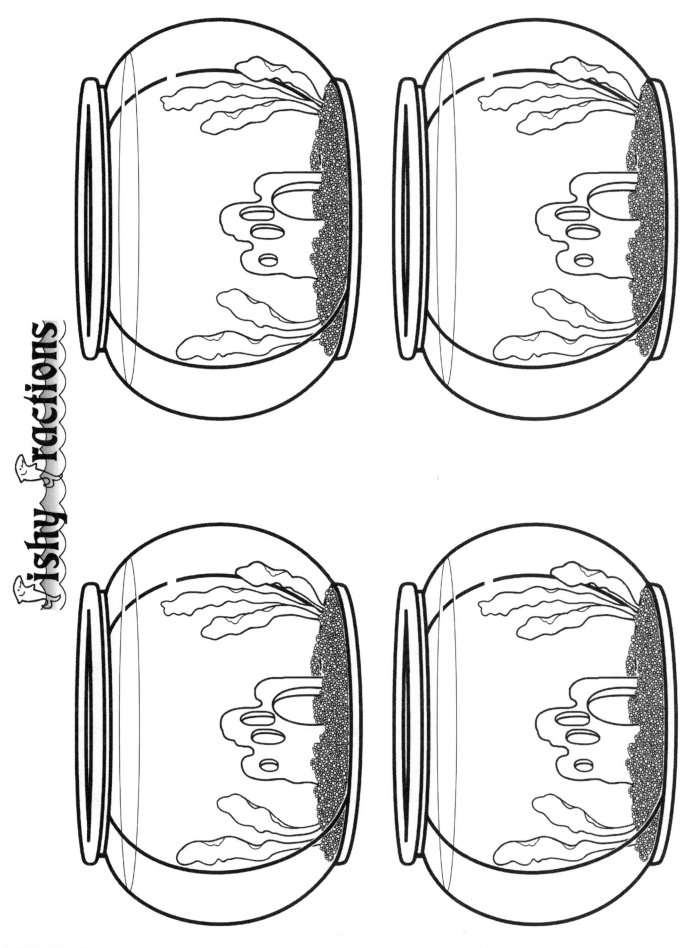

Fishy Fractions

Color these fish red, orange, yellow, green, and purple.

SOLVE IT! 2nd   53   © 2005 AIMS Education Foundation

CARD COMBOS

Topic
Number sense

Key Question
How can manipulating a set of number cards help you learn about numbers?

Learning Goal
Students will use a set of number cards to solve problems involving place value, ordering, and equalities and inequalities.

Guiding Document
*NCTM Standards 2000**
* *Develop a sense of whole numbers and represent and use them in flexible ways, including relating, composing, and decomposing numbers*
* *Use multiple models to develop initial understandings of place value and the base-ten number system*
* *Build new mathematical knowledge through problem solving*
* *Solve problems that arise in mathematics and in other contexts*

Math
Number sense and numeration
Ordering
Equalities and inequalities
Problem solving

Integrated Processes
Observing
Comparing and contrasting

Problem-Solving Strategy
Use manipulatives

Materials
Number cards (see *Management 1*)

Background Information
It is important for young learners to use manipulatives such as counting bears, beans, etc., to solve word problems and develop mathematical vocabulary. This allows them to act out the problems in a very concrete way. In this activity, the objects being manipulated will be the numbers 0-9. Due to the abstract nature of numbers, it is suggested that the students have a good understanding of the numbers 0-9 and the sets that they represent prior to participating in this lesson.

The activity was designed to give students an opportunity to review a variety of math skills using a manipulative. A set of suggested questions has been provided; however, we recommend that you create additional questions that will meet your local standards and students' needs.

Management
1. Copy one set of the number cards 0-9 onto card stock for each student. You can also have each student make his or her own set of number cards by writing the numbers 0-9 on scratch paper or sticky notes.
2. Remind the students to place all of their cards back together after each problem.

Procedure
1. Distribute one set of number cards to each student.
2. Read the following instructions and questions aloud to your students. Some students may need the problems repeated.
   * I am thinking of a number that is odd. It is more than 6 and less than 9. What is my number?
   * Take the 1, 2, and 3 number cards. What is the largest two-digit number you can make? [32] What number is in the tens place? How many ones do you have?
   * How can you change the number 16 into 61? Explain.
   * Make the numbers 23 and 45. Use a greater than, less than, or equal to sign to show the relationship between the numbers.
   * Show me a number, that when I subtract 2 from it, I get a number larger than 5.
   * Take the number 4, 3, and 1 cards. Make a number that falls between 30 and 40.
   * Show me the number 135. Which digit is in the hundreds place? ...tens place? ... ones place?
   * Take the number 4, 3, and 1 cards. Make a number that falls between 100 and 150. What number did you make? What digit is in the tens place? Are there any other possibilities?
   * Take the number 1, 2, and 3 cards. What are all of the possible two- and three-digit numbers that you can make with these three cards?

- Make the numbers 189 and 234. Which one is greater? Use a greater than, less than, or equal to sign to show the relationship between the two numbers.
- Make the number 121. What numbers does it fall between? Is it closer to 120 or 130?
- What two numbers when added together would give me eight? Are there any other possibilities?
- Show me a number larger than 10 and smaller than 20 that becomes a number larger than 60 and smaller than 70 when its digits are reversed.
- What is the largest odd number you can make using the numbers 3, 8, and 9? ...the smallest odd number?
- What is the largest even number you can make using the numbers 2, 4, and 7? ...the smallest even number?

Connecting Learning
1. How did you decide if the number you built was odd or even?
2. How did you know which number was in the ones, tens, and hundreds place?
3. How did you decide which number was larger when comparing numbers?
4. How did the number cards help you solve problems?

Extension
Have students create their own problems for the class to solve using the set of number cards.

* Reprinted with permission from *Principles and Standards for School Mathematics*, 2000 by the National Council of Teachers of Mathematics. All rights reserved

4	9
3	8
2	7
1	6
0	5

Sweet Squares

Topic
Measurement

Key Question
How can we use square, fruit-flavored candy to measure birthday cards?

Learning Goals
Students will:
1. find the length and width of birthday cards,
2. find the area of birthday cards, and
3. find the perimeter of birthday cards.

Guiding Document
*NCTM Standards 2000**
- *Recognize the attributes of length, volume, weight, area, and time*
- *Compare and order objects according to these attributes*
- *Understand how to measure using nonstandard and standard units*
- *Count with understanding and recognize "how many" in sets of objects*
- *Measure with multiple copies of units of the same size, such as paper clips laid end to end*
- *Use repetition of a single unit to measure something larger than the unit, for instance, measuring the length of a room with a single meterstick*
- *Develop common referents for measures to make comparisons and estimates*
- *Build new mathematical knowledge through problem solving*
- *Solve problems that arise in mathematics and in other contexts*

Math
Measurement
  linear
  area
  perimeter
Estimation
Problem solving

Integrated Processes
Observing
Predicting
Collecting and recording data

Problem-Solving Strategy
Use manipulatives

Materials
Birthday cards (see *Management 1*)
Square, fruit-flavored candies (see *Management 2*)
Student pages

Background information
Students should begin measuring using non-customary units. Fruit candy squares provide a standard unit that is playful and will transition well to customary units. Linear measurement is probably familiar to most students. Square units are a standard unit of measure; however, many students have not had opportunities to work with them.

Management
1. Square and rectangular cards work the best. Students can either use their own birthday cards or the page of birthday card illustrations provided. Students will need to round measurements to the nearest whole candy unit.
2. *Parts One* and *Two* of this activity should be done individually and *Part Three* should be done in pairs. Each individual will need 10 square, fruit-flavored candies, and each pair will need 20.

Procedure
Part One—Linear Measurement
1. Hold up two birthday cards and ask students which card is larger. Record their responses on the board. Ask the students how they could find out which one is actually larger. [Students may suggest directly comparing the two cards by placing one on the other. If they do, follow up by asking how much bigger the larger card is.]
2. Invite two students to the front of the class. Give one of the birthday cards to each student. Explain that they will be measuring using square candy units. Ask the students to measure the heights of their cards in candy units. On the board, write *card one* and *card two*. Record the height measurements of the cards. Discuss which card is taller and by how much.
3. Invite two additional students to measure the widths of the cards in candy units. Record and discuss this information.

SOLVE IT! 2nd   57   © 2005 AIMS Education Foundation

4. Ask students to choose two birthday cards and determine the heights and widths of their cards in candy units. Have the students record the measurements on the student page. Ask the students to compare the two cards and make a true statement about their measurements. For example, "My giraffe card is two candy units taller than my cake card."
5. Have students choose two additional cards. Ask them to measure the additional cards and place them in order from shortest to tallest based on the height measurements. Discuss their findings.

Part Two—Area
1. Remind students of how they previously used candy units to measure the heights and widths of their birthday cards. Explain that in this experience, they will be covering the entire card with candy units to find the area of the card.
2. Hold up a birthday card and ask students to estimate how many square candies it would take to cover the card. Record their responses on the board.
3. Invite a student to come forward and find the actual number by covering the card with candy squares. Discuss the relationship between the estimations and the actual area.
4. Ask students to select one of their cards. Have them find the area of the card in square candy units and record the area on their student pages. Discuss who had the card with the largest area, the smallest area, etc. Lead the students to make the generalization that the larger the area, the larger the card.
5. Direct the students to choose a card that they predict would have a larger area than the first card they measured. Have them record the measurements on their student page. Ask them to make a true statement comparing the area of the two cards.

Part Three—Perimeter
1. Remind students of the two previous experiences they have had measuring with candy units.
2. Discuss the concept of perimeter.
3. Together, determine the perimeter of a variety of items in the classroom—such as a book or the desk top—in candy units.
4. Explain to students that they will now be working in pairs using candy units to determine the perimeters of their cards. Have the students record their results on the student page. Discuss their findings.

Connecting Learning
1. How is a candy unit like other units we measure with? How is it different?
2. What did you do when a card didn't measure in whole candy units? [rounded to the nearest whole candy unit]
3. Was it difficult to measure the heights and widths of any of your cards? Why or why not? [If cards could not be measured in whole candy units, needing to round may have made things more difficult.]
4. When is it important to know the length, width, area, and perimeter of things?
5. What could we use instead of candy units to find the height, width, area, and perimeter of the cards?

Curriculum Correlation
Murphy, Stuart. *Big Better Best.* HarperCollins. New York. 2002.

* Reprinted with permission from *Principles and Standards for School Mathematics, 2000* by the National Council of Teachers of Mathematics. All rights reserved.

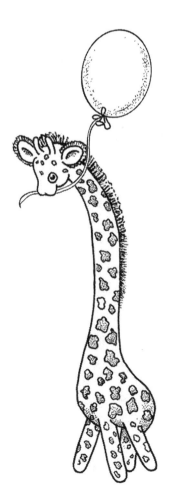

Sweet Squares

Part One—Height and Width

Card One
Height: _____ Width: _____

Card Two
Height: _____ Width: _____

Write about the measurements of your cards.

_____

_____

_____

_____

On the back of this page, place your four cards in order from shortest to tallest. Then trace your cards and write the height measurement on each.

Part Two—Area

Trace the cards you chose on the back of the paper.

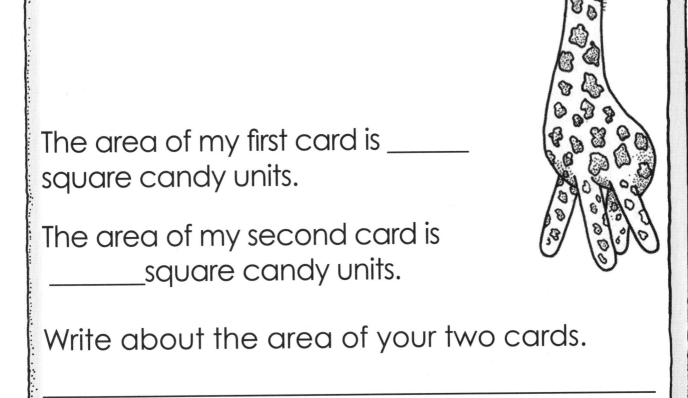

The area of my first card is _____ square candy units.

The area of my second card is _____ square candy units.

Write about the area of your two cards.

_____
_____
_____

Sweet Squares

Part Three—Perimeter

The perimeter of _____
(describe what you measured)
is _____ candy units.

We measured our _____
(describe the card)
birthday card. The perimeter was _____ candy units.

We measured our _____
(describe the card)
birthday card. The perimeter was _____ candy units.

It is larger/smaller than the first one we measured.
(circle one)

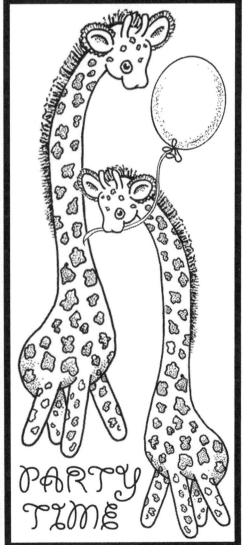

Problem-Solving Strategies
Draw out the Problem

Drawing a picture is an effective problem-solving tool for young children. This strategy allows them to "see" the problem as they represent relevant information, and it gives them a concrete way to justify their responses. However, it is important to stress to students that the pictures do not need to be elaborate. This strategy is useful when the problem requires all of the necessary information to be represented in order for a solution to be determined.

Counting Clues

Topic
Problem solving

Key Question
How can drawing pictures help us solve mathematical problems?

Learning Goal
Students will draw pictures to solve word problems.

Guiding Document
*NCTM Standards 2000**
- *Develop a sense of whole numbers and represent and use them in flexible ways, including relating, composing, and decomposing numbers*
- *Understand the effects of adding and subtracting whole numbers*
- *Count with understanding and recognize "how many" in sets of objects*
- *Build new mathematical knowledge through problem solving*
- *Solve problems that arise in mathematics and in other contexts*
- *Apply and adapt a variety of appropriate strategies to solve problems*

Math
Whole number operations
    addition
    subtraction
Problem solving

Integrated Processes
Observing
Comparing and contrasting
Relating

Problem-Solving Strategy
Draw out the problem

Materials
Crayons
Scratch paper
Set of clue cards (see *Management 1*)
Sticky notes

Background Information
    Drawing a picture is an effective problem-solving tool for young children. This strategy allows them to represent relevant information and gives them a concrete way to justify their responses. This activity provides the students with the type of problem where they naturally want to draw a picture in order to find an accurate solution.

Management
1. Copy one set of the counting cards onto transparencies to be used on the overhead.
2. The counting clue cards can be used one at a time over several days as a "bright beginning" to start math for the day, or used as a complete set for an entire class period.
3. Before placing the clue card onto the overhead, cover the pictures with sticky notes so that the students only see the problem.

Procedure
1. Distribute crayons and scratch paper to each student.
2. Explain to the students that you will be placing a problem on the overhead for them to solve. Remind them that they are allowed to use scratch paper to help them solve the problems.
3. Place one clue card on the overhead with the picture covered. Allow time for the class to find a solution.
4. When the students have had ample time to solve the problem, discuss their solutions. Question them about the strategies they used to find their answers. If a student says that they drew a picture, reveal the picture on the card, and suggest that drawing a picture is how you would also go about solving the problem. Repeat this process each time you present *Counting Clues* problems.

Connecting Learning
1. How did you solve the *Counting Clues* problems?
2. How can drawing pictures help you in math?
3. Which problems were the easiest to solve? Why?
4. Which problems were the hardest to solve? Why?

Extension
Have students write their own counting clues and exchange them with their classmates.

* Reprinted with permission from *Principles and Standards for School Mathematics*, 2000 by the National Council of Teachers of Mathematics. All rights reserved

Counting Clues

Stop and Go

How many letters are in the words stop and go?

What is the number of ears on three bunnies with fluffy tails?

How many legs are on three cows and two chickens?

How many fingers do two boys and a little girl with blond hair have?

SOLVE IT! 2nd © 2005 AIMS Education Foundation

Counting Clues

How many eyes are on four fish?

How many feet do three frogs have?

How many wheels are on two cars and three bicycles?

Six nests. The first three nests have three eggs. The other three nests have two eggs. How many eggs?

Counting Clues

Three flowers with two leaves and five petals each. How many leaves? How many petals?

How many bows on two red packages and three blue packages?

Four bears. How many noses?

Three blind mice. How many tails?

Counting Clues

How many digits in your phone number?

Four kids. How many feet?

How many hands on four clocks?

Two ducks and three dogs. How many legs?

Topic
Problem solving

Key Question
How can you figure out the answers to the number riddles?

Learning Goal
Students will use their problem-solving skills to determine the answer to number riddles.

Guiding Document
NCTM Standards 2000*
- *Build new mathematical knowledge through problem solving*
- *Apply and adapt a variety of appropriate strategies to solve problems*

Math
Logic
Computation
Problem solving

Integrated Processes
Observing
Analyzing
Recording

Problem-Solving Strategies
Draw out the problem
Use logical thinking
Use manipulatives

Materials
Student pages
Manipulatives, optional

Background Information
A-counting for Apples is a series of riddles, all centered on apples, that challenges students to perform basic computation, to recognize necessary information, and to discard distracting details. All these skills are necessary for solving word problems, a skill required on many standardized tests. Students will be able to employ a variety of problem-solving skills—including drawing out the problem, using logical thinking, and using manipulatives—as they solve the riddles.

Management
1. Because of the abstract nature of the riddles, students will likely want to draw out the problems or use manipulatives to solve them. You can provide appropriate manipulatives if desired.
2. The first page of riddles is fairly simple, while the second page is somewhat more challenging. You will need to gauge the abilities of your students when determining which parts of the activity are appropriate.

Procedure
1. Distribute the student page(s) and explain the task to the class.
2. Give students time to read the problems and come up with the solutions.
3. Close with a time of class discussion and sharing.

Connecting Learning
1. What problem-solving strategies did you use to help you solve the problems?
2. Did you use the same strategy on every problem? Why or why not?
3. How do these strategies compare to the ones used by your classmates?
4. Were some problems easier to solve than others? Explain.

Extension
Allow students to come up with their own apple riddles.

* Reprinted with permission from *Principles and Standards for School Mathematics,* 2000 by the National Council of Teachers of Mathematics. All rights reserved.

SOLVE IT! 2nd © 2005 AIMS Education Foundation

A-Counting for Apples

The red apple has fewer than 10 seeds and more than 8 seeds. How many seeds does the apple have?

The number of apples on the tree is five more than the number of fingers and toes on your teacher. How many apples are on the tree?

The number of apple baskets is the same as the number of legs on the gray cat and the brown dog. How many apple baskets are there?

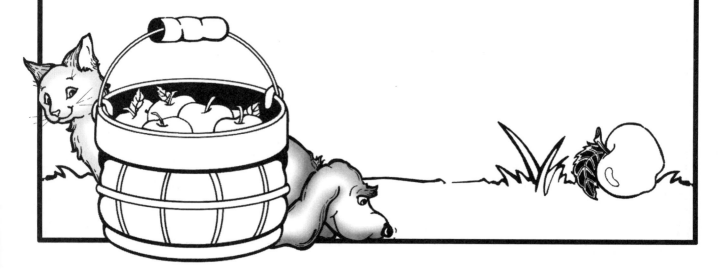

The number of trees in the orchard is
more than 20, but less than 30.
Both of the digits in the number of trees are the same.
How many trees are in the orchard?

There are 12 apples total. Some are red,
some are yellow, and some are green.
Four of the apples are red and three are green.
How many apples are yellow?

Yesterday morning, there were 9 apples on the tree.
This morning, the crows came and ate 2 apples.
This afternoon, some apples fell off the tree
Now there are 3 apples on the tree.
How many fell off?

Picturing a Solution

Topic
Problem solving

Key Question
How can you solve word problems by drawing out the problem?

Learning Goal
Students will solve word problems by drawing pictures.

Guiding Document
*NCTM Standards 2000**
- Apply and adapt a variety of appropriate strategies to solve problems
- Build new mathematical knowledge through problem solving

Math
Counting
Problem solving

Integrated Processes
Observing
Recording
Applying

Problem-Solving Strategy
Draw out the problem

Materials
Paper for drawing
Colored pencils or crayons, optional

Background Information
A powerful problem-solving tool at the primary grades is drawing out the problem. This strategy allows students to represent all of the necessary information and gives them a concrete way to justify their responses. This activity simply presents several word problems that can be solved most easily by drawing out the problem.

Management
1. Students should be allowed to work together in collaborative pairs on this task.
2. You may want to put some of the word problems at a center where students can work on them individually or in small groups.

Procedure
1. Read a problem to the class. You may also wish to write it on the board so that students can continue to refer to it as they draw their pictures.
2. Give groups time to draw out the problem and determine a solution.
3. Allow groups to share their answers and how they got those answers.
4. Repeat this process with the additional problems.

Word Problems
1. Three friends were painting their fingernails and toenails.
   Two girls painted their fingernails pink.
   One girl painted her toenails pink.
   How many nails were not pink?
2. Five boys were playing in a pool.
   Two were splashing using their hands and feet.
   One was splashing using only his hands.
   One was splashing using only his feet.
   How many hands and feet were not splashing?
3. Six kittens were playing inside.
   Two got their front paws tangled in yarn.
   Three got their back paws tangled in yarn.
   How many paws were not tangled?
4. Anna has two brothers and two sisters. They are all wearing shorts and shirts.
   Today both of her brothers had their shirts on inside out.
   One of her sisters had her shorts on backwards.
   How many shirts and shorts were on correctly?

Connecting Learning
1. How did drawing out the picture help you answer the problems?
2. What are some other ways that you could have solved these problems?
3. Do you think that these other ways would be harder or easier than drawing the problem? Why?

Extensions
1. As students become comfortable with the process, they can be challenged to develop their own problems for classmates to solve.
2. Challenge students to use manipulatives to represent the parts of the problem rather than drawing each one out.

* Reprinted with permission from *Principles and Standards for School Mathematics*, 2000 by the National Council of Teachers of Mathematics. All rights reserved.

Problem-Solving Strategies
Write a Number Sentence

When dealing with word problems or similar challenges, it is often beneficial to simply write down the numbers and operation symbols needed to solve the problem. Writing the number sentence helps students organize the information so that they can see if the numbers and operations used correspond to the information given and if the answer makes sense.

Telling Tales

Topic
Problem solving

Key Question
How can writing number sentences help us solve problems?

Learning Goal
Students will write number sentences that describe what is displayed in various fairy tale pictures.

Guiding Document
NCTM Standards 2000*
- *Develop a sense of whole numbers and represent and use them in flexible ways, including relating, composing, and decomposing numbers*
- *Understand the effects of adding and subtracting whole numbers*
- *Build new mathematical knowledge through problem solving*
- *Solve problems that arise in mathematics and in other contexts*
- *Apply and adapt a variety of appropriate strategies to solve problems*
- *Monitor and reflect on the process of mathematical problem solving*

Math
Number and operations
   addition
   subtraction
Problem solving

Problem-Solving Strategy
Write a number sentence

Integrated Processes
Observing
Comparing and contrasting
Collecting and recording data
Interpreting data

Materials
Fairy tale pictures (see *Management 1*)
Student pages

Background Information
Sometimes one of the most useful problem-solving strategies is to simply write down the numbers and operation symbols you need to use to solve a problem. This helps students organize the information so they can see if the operation they selected makes sense with the numbers in the problem. However, for young children to truly understand the effects of adding and subtracting whole numbers, it is important for them to see pictures or manipulate objects. This allows them to develop visual images of both the data in the problem and the solution process. When children are encouraged to describe and represent quantities in different ways, they also learn to recognize equivalent representations and expand their ability to use symbols to communicate their thinking.

Management
1. Prior to the lesson, make one copy of the fairy tale pictures for each pair of students on card stock. The pictures can be enlarged, colored, and laminated for extended use. Enlarged, they can be used with the entire class or placed in a center. Also, make one copy of the Cinderella picture on transparency film to use on the overhead projector.
2. Make one copy of each student page per student.
3. It is suggested that students first make observations about what they see in the picture. This will help students when it comes time for them to write their own questions and number sentences.
4. All four pictures can be used in one math period, or they can be spread out over several days after the initial instruction.

Procedure
1. Place the transparency of Cinderella and Prince Charming on the overhead.
2. Ask the students to observe the picture and describe what they see in detail. For example, there are two white mice and three gray mice, etc.
3. When the class has demonstrated an awareness of the details in the picture, tell them that you will be asking them some questions about the picture and that you would like them to write a number sentence to help them answer the questions.

SOLVE IT! 2nd   © 2005 AIMS Education Foundation

4. Ask the class how many shoelaces are in the picture. Invite a student to come to the board and write the number sentence that would help us answer the question. [1 + 1 + 1 + 1 = 4, or 2 + 2 = 4 would be correct responses]. Ask the student to explain his or her thinking. Repeat the process asking questions about the number of noses, arms, etc.
5. Distribute the pictures and student pages and tell the class that you would like them to write a number sentence for two additional questions. Then challenge the students to come up with an additional number sentence that would describe the picture. Remind students to label their problems so that you can understand them. For example, 2 eyes + 2 eyes = 4 eyes, etc.
6. Provide time for discussion and for students to share their number sentences.

Connecting Learning
1. How did writing number sentences help you solve the problems?
2. How did you know whether the number sentence should be addition or subtraction?
3. Show me what 1 + 5 = 6 might look like in picture form.
4. If I describe a picture that has 12 black cats and three white cats and ask you how many cats are in the picture, what number sentence would you write?

Extensions
1. Gather a collection of fairy tale books, display a picture from one of the books, and see how many different number sentences can describe the picture.
2. Write several word problems on sentence strips and place them in a pocket chart. Ask the students what pictures they would visualize and what number sentences they would write to solve the problems.

* Reprinted with permission from *Principles and Standards for School Mathematics*, 2000 by the National Council of Teachers of Mathematics. All rights reserved.

SOLVE IT! 2nd   76   © 2005 AIMS Education Foundation

1. How many shoes?

2. How many mice?

3. What other number sentences describe this picture?

1. How many candy canes?

2. How many peppermints?

3. What other number sentences describe this picture?

1. How many fingers?

2. If Snow White and one dwarf fall asleep, how many people will be awake?

3. What other number sentences describe this picture?

1. How many eggs?

2. How many beans?

3. What other number sentences describe this picture?

Frog Tales

Topic
Whole number operations

Key Question
How can we use a storyboard to act out mathematical problems?

Learning Goals
Students will:
1. use their own words to describe experiences in a mathematical setting,
2. use manipulatives to represent number stories, and
3. write number sentences that describe what is being acted out on their storyboards

Guiding Document
NCTM Standards 2000*
- *Develop a sense of whole numbers and represent and use them in flexible ways, including relating, composing, and decomposing numbers*
- *Count with understanding and recognize "how many" in sets of objects*
- *Understand the effects of adding and subtracting whole numbers*
- *Understand situations that entail multiplication and division, such as equal groupings of objects and sharing equally*
- *Model situations that involve the addition and subtraction of whole numbers, using objects, pictures, and symbols*
- *Apply and adapt a variety of appropriate strategies to solve problems*
- *Build new mathematical knowledge through problem solving*
- *Solve problems that arise in mathematics and in other contexts*

Math
Counting
Whole number operations
    addition
    subtraction
Problem solving

Integrated Processes
Observing
Comparing and contrasting
Relating

Problem-Solving Strategies
Write a number sentence
Use manipulatives
Act out the problem

Materials
Storyboard (see *Management 1*)
Plastic frogs (see *Management 2*)
Scratch paper
Large number cards (see *Management 3*)
Card stock

Background Information
This activity focuses on the problem-solving strategy of writing a number sentence to solve story problems. Often, older students will look for key words or phrases in a story problem such as "how many are left," or "how many are there in all," to help them identify the appropriate operation, then write the number sentence and solve the problem. However, for young children it is often helpful to use objects such as the frogs in this activity to act out the problem. This allows them to visualize the joining together (addition) process and the taking apart (subtraction) process.

The goal of this activity is for students to transition from acting out problems to writing number sentences to solve problems. Students will act out the problems using plastic or paper frogs, assign numbers to the sets of frogs, and decide on the appropriate operation symbol to create a number sentence.

Management
1. The storyboard can be enlarged, colored, and laminated for extended use. Enlarged, it is ideal to use in a flannel board format in front of the class. It can also be copied onto an overhead transparency and displayed using an overhead projector.
2. Small plastic frogs can be obtained through The Oriental Trading Company (1-800-228-2269, http://www.oriental.com), Discount School Supply (1-800-627-2829, http://www.earlychildhood.com), or your local department store. If plastic frogs are not available, copy the page of frogs provided for each student.
3. On 8.5" x 11" pieces of card stock, write the numbers zero through nine, a plus sign, a minus sign, and an equal sign. Use these large number cards to display in the chalk tray at the front of the room.

SOLVE IT! 2nd   © 2005 AIMS Education Foundation

Procedure
1. Give each child a set of 15 frogs and a storyboard, or invite the students to come to the front of the class where you have an enlarged version.
2. Have students describe what they see on the storyboard.
3. Read one of the suggested problems aloud to your students. Then read it again while they act it out with the frogs either on their boards or in front of the class with the enlarged version. Some students may need to listen to the story several times while they solve the problem.
4. Once students have their storyboards arranged, have them write a number sentence that describes the story on a piece of scratch paper.
5. Once everyone has recorded a number sentence, have a volunteer come to the front of the class and arrange the number cards to show a number sentence describing the story.
6. Have the class compare the number sentences they wrote to the one at the front of the class. In instances where more than one number sentence is appropriate, have other students use the large number cards to show additional possibilities.
7. Tell the students to clear their boards and repeat the process with additional questions.

Suggested Problems
- Rakisha has 11 frogs in her pond and Elora gives her four more. How many frogs does Rakisha have? Tell us about your picture. (Addition, Combining)
- Three red and yellow frogs are in the water, two more are on the large lily pad, and one is on the small lily pad. How many frogs are there altogether? (Addition, Combining)
- Maria has five striped frogs in her pond. Nora has seven spotted frogs on her log. Are there more frogs in Maria's pond or on Nora's log? How many more? (Subtraction, Comparison Model)
- There were four blue frogs in the water and five black frogs on the bank. A very strong breeze came along and blew three of the frogs off the bank and into the water. How many frogs were left on the bank? How many are now in the water? (Subtraction, Take-away Model)
- Raphael found three frogs in the cattails, Kari found two frogs in the water, Jamar found five frogs on the log, and Aree found no frogs. How many frogs did the four friends find altogether? (Addition, Combining)
- There are three frogs in the water. There are two more frogs on the bank than in the water. How many frogs are on the bank? (Subtraction, Take-Away Model)
- Seven frogs are in the water. Five are put onto Deo's log. How many are in the water? How many are on the log? (Missing Addend)
- Nicholas has two frogs on each lily pad. How many frogs does he have altogether? (Addition, Combining)
- Vang had nine frogs. He wanted to put an equal number on each of the three lily pads. How many will be on each lily pad? (Division)
- If Tamilia has 10 frogs, can she divide them evenly onto three lily pads? How many would be on each lily pad? How many would be left over? (Division)

Connecting Learning
1. Did the storyboards help you solve problems? Explain.
2. How did you know when to add and when to subtract the frogs?
3. How did you solve the problem with 10 frogs being divided evenly among three lily pads?
4. Which problems were hardest for you to solve? Why? Which were easiest?
5. If you know that there are five frogs, some are in the water and some are on the log, how many different pictures can you make?
6. How did you know what number sentence to write for each story?
7. Were there times when more than one number sentence was possible? Give an example.

Extension
Have your students create their own storyboards and math questions to go with them.

Curriculum Correlation
Butler, Christina M. *Too Many Eggs*. David R. Godine Publisher. Boston. 1994.

Crews, Donald. *Ten Black Dots*. HarperTrophy. New York. 1995.

Sis, Peter. *Waving*. Greenwillow Books. New York. 1988.

* Reprinted with permission from *Principles and Standards for School Mathematics*, 2000 by the National Council of Teachers of Mathematics. All rights reserved.

Exploring Operations Through Storyboards

Creation/Recognition of a Set
Given a number the child will build a set to represent the number, or given a group of objects the child will count the members of the set.

Comparison of Sets
The concepts of *more, less,* and *the same as* are basic relationships that are essential to develop meaning in operations. The child should construct sets to show these relationships using manipulatives, as well as make comparisons or choices between two given sets.

Composition/Decomposition of Sets (Part-Part-Whole)
Children either build a designated quantity in two or more parts, or they begin with a designated amount and separate it into two or more parts.

Addition of Sets: Combining (Part-Part-Whole)
To learn what joining a set of two (a part) and a set of three (a part) means, the child must manipulate two objects and three objects and combine to make a set of five objects (the whole).

Addition: Comparison Model
If the smaller of two sets and the difference between them are known, then addition tells how many are in the larger set. A real-world example would be Sally saying to Patty, "I have three more pennies than you have," and Patty knows that she is holding two pennies. Addition tells how many Sally has.

Subtraction: Take-away Model (Whole-Part-Part)
The child creates a set of a designated amount (the whole) and is asked to take away an amount (a part) and identify what is left (a part).

Subtraction: Comparison Model
The child creates two sets, compares them, and identifies the difference between them.

Missing Addend (Whole-Part-Part)
The child creates a set (the whole) and must cover up or hide some of the set (a part). The child is encouraged to "think addition," or to answer the question: "What goes with the remaining pieces (a part) to make the whole amount?"

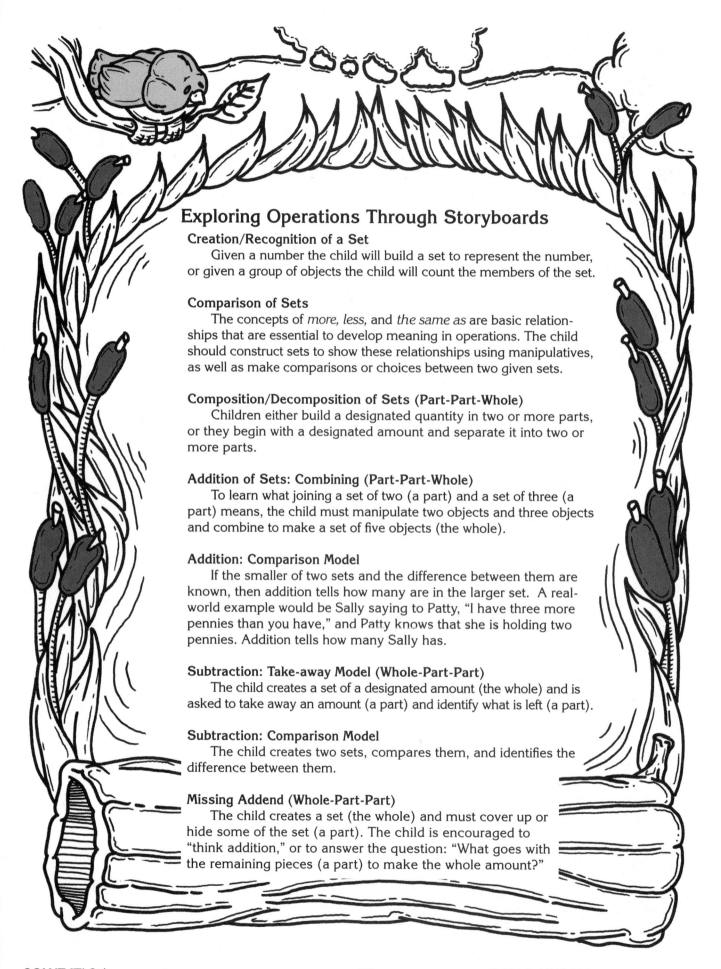

Equation Creation

Topic
Whole number operations

Key Question
How can you complete the equation started by your partner?

Learning Goals
Students will:
1. determine multiple ways to complete equations started by their partners,
2. record their solutions, and
3. look for patterns in those solutions to help understand the inverse nature of addition and subtraction.

Guiding Document
NCTM Standards 2000*
- *Develop fluency with basic number combinations for addition and subtraction*
- *Develop and use strategies for whole-number computations, with a focus on addition and subtraction*
- *Understand the effects of adding and subtracting whole numbers*
- *Understand various meanings of addition and subtraction of whole numbers and the relationship between the two operations*
- *Model situations that involve the addition and subtraction of whole numbers, using objects, pictures, and symbols*
- *Illustrate general principles and properties of operations, such as commutativity, using specific numbers*
- *Build new mathematical knowledge through problem solving*

Math
Whole number operations
　　addition
　　subtraction
Number sense
Problem solving

Integrated Processes
Observing
Recording
Generalizing

Problem-Solving Strategies
Write a number sentence
Use manipulatives
Work backwards
Look for patterns

Materials
Number cards
Recording page

Background Information
　　This problem is rich in both its number and problem-solving content. The context of a game provides a playful, engaging setting in which children can explore concepts of the commutativity of addition, the inverse nature of addition and subtraction, fact families, equations, and more. While none of these terms needs to be used with the students, the concepts they represent are important, and should be addressed through the discussion following the activity. As they do this activity, students will be exercising multiple problem-solving skills, including writing a number sentence, using manipulatives, and working backwards.
　　In the game, students are challenged to complete equations begun by another student by placing the correct numbers on the other side of the equal sign. We often use the term "number sentence" instead of equation, but this causes us to lose a valuable opportunity to expose young children to the language of algebraic thinking. Any time a problem is written horizontally and contains an equal sign, it is an equation. This concept is fundamental to later learning in algebra when students will solve for x by subtracting, dividing, etc., the same thing from both sides of an equation.

Management
1. Students need to work in pairs on this activity. Each pair needs one set of number cards. They can cut these apart themselves, or you can do it for them ahead of time. For greater durability, laminate the cards.
2. Number cards are provided for the numbers zero through nine. If you wish to reduce the difficulty of this activity, take out the higher numbers. For a greater challenge, add numbers greater than nine.

SOLVE IT! 2ⁿᵈ　　　　　　　　　　© 2005 AIMS Education Foundation

Procedure

Part One
1. Before having students play the game in pairs, play a few sample rounds as a class. Write _____ + _____ = 3 on the board. Invite a student to come up and fill in the blanks to make the equation true.
2. Ask if anyone else can come up with another way to make the equation true. Invite another student to come up and write a second equation using different numbers to sum to three. See if there are any other students who think they have different ways to make two numbers add up to three. Allow them to write their answers on the board and discuss how many solutions there are for the problem.
3. Discuss how some of the answers use the same numbers, they are just in a different order. Decide as a class whether or not you will accept answers using the same numbers in a different order as unique.
4. Repeat this process using a subtraction problem.

Part Two
1. Once students are comfortable with the concept, tell them that they will be playing a version of this game with a partner.
2. Have students get into pairs and distribute the number cards and recording page. Depending on the number of equations you want students to find, you may need to provide multiple copies of the recording page.
3. Explain that one person in each pair will begin by putting out either a plus or minus sign, an equal sign, and one number card to the right of the equal sign. The other person must pick two of the remaining number cards to make the equation true.
4. If both partners agree that the equation is correct, have them record it in the appropriate place on their student pages. (One student will write it in the *My Equations* column, the other will write it in the *My Partner's Equations* column.)
5. Have students take turns creating and recording different equations for the same sum or difference until neither can find any more. The rules decided upon as a class govern whether answers that use the same two numbers in a different order are acceptable.
6. When partners have exhausted the combinations for one number, have them switch roles with the other player beginning a different equation using a new number and either a plus or minus sign.
7. Repeat this process as time allows, or for a specified number of equations.
8. At the end of the activity, have each student count his or her total number of equations. The player with the most is the winner.

Connecting Learning

1. How many equations did you find for a sum of seven? ...a difference of two?
2. Do you think you have found them all? Why or why not?
3. Which numbers had the most possible equations when you were adding? Which numbers had the fewest? Why?
4. Which numbers had the most possible equations when you were subtracting? Which numbers had the fewest? Why?
5. Did any numbers have the same number of possible equations for adding and subtracting? Why do you think this is?
6. When you look at your equations, do you see any patterns in the equations?
7. What do the equations tell you about how addition and subtraction are related?
8. How did writing these equations help you to see that relationship?
9. What are you wondering now?

Extensions

1. Have students organize their equations in some kind of order and look for patterns.
2. Add a second addition sign and have students explore three-number sums.

* Reprinted with permission from *Principles and Standards for School Mathematics*, 2000 by the National Council of Teachers of Mathematics. All rights reserved.

Equation Creation

My Equations	My Partner's Equations
___ + ___ = ___	___ + ___ = ___
___ + ___ = ___	___ + ___ = ___
___ + ___ = ___	___ + ___ = ___
___ + ___ = ___	___ + ___ = ___
___ + ___ = ___	___ + ___ = ___
___ + ___ = ___	___ + ___ = ___
___ + ___ = ___	___ + ___ = ___
___ + ___ = ___	___ + ___ = ___

My Equations   My Partner's Equations

___ − ___ = ___   ___ − ___ = ___

___ − ___ = ___   ___ − ___ = ___

___ − ___ = ___   ___ − ___ = ___

___ − ___ = ___   ___ − ___ = ___

___ − ___ = ___   ___ − ___ = ___

___ − ___ = ___   ___ − ___ = ___

___ − ___ = ___   ___ − ___ = ___

___ − ___ = ___   ___ − ___ = ___

1	2	3	4
5	6	7	8
9	0	1	2
3	4	5	6
7	8	9	0
+	−	=	

Problem-Solving Strategies
Use Logical Thinking

Using logical thinking as a problem-solving strategy involves combining information and using deductive and inductive reasoning to explain why a solution is valid. In many cases, inferences must be made to fill in missing information. Sometimes a grid is used to organize the clues. Other times manipulatives represent the parts of the problem. This strategy is used when multiple pieces of information need to be combined to arrive at an answer.

Seasonal Logic

Topic
Logic

Key Question
How can you use the clues and logical thinking to solve a series of problems?

Learning Goal
Students will use logical thinking to solve a series of problems.

Guiding Document
NCTM Standards 2000*
* *Build new mathematical knowledge through problem solving*
* *Solve problems that arise in mathematics and in other contexts*
* *Monitor and reflect on the process of mathematical problem solving*
* *Apply and adapt a variety of appropriate strategies to solve problems*

Math
Logic
Problem solving

Integrated Processes
Observing
Comparing and contrasting
Collecting and recording data
Interpreting data

Problem-Solving Strategies
Use logical thinking
Use manipulatives

Materials
Transparencies
Transparency pen
Small manipulatives
Student pages

Background Information
Using logical thinking as a problem-solving strategy involves examining a set of clues and using deductive and inductive reasoning to explain why a solution is valid. Often in logic problems a grid is used to organize these clues. There are several ways to go about solving logic problems. It is important to expose the students to different strategies and allow them to choose the one that they are most comfortable with.

Some students find it helpful to use an X and checkmark system to keep track of the information gathered from each clue while others prefer to use manipulatives on the grid to help them solve the logic problems.

With the X and checkmark system, students read a clue and place an X in any box(es) that can be eliminated based on the clue and a checkmark in any box that is correct based on the clue.

When using manipulatives to solve logic problems, students place one manipulative in each space on the grid. Manipulatives are removed as the options they represent are eliminated, and those that remain identify correct answers. Whatever process is used, students should test their conclusions against the clues, making adjustments until they are satisfied with the solutions they have found.

Management
1. This activity contains eight seasonal logic problems for use at different times throughout the school year. There are problems for the beginning of school, fall, Thanksgiving, December holidays, winter, Valentine's Day, Easter, and spring. Use the appropriate problems at the appropriate times.
2. First-time exposure to simple logic problems will require a highly structured, teacher-directed experience. When students are familiar with the process, they can work in pairs or small groups.
3. Make a transparency of the *Back to School—One* page grid.
4. If your students have never worked with linear logic problems before, you may want to enlarge the pictures of the eggs, pumpkins, and snowflakes so that they each fill a page. Four students can hold these pages at the front of the class while the other students move them around based on the clues to arrive at the solution.

Procedure
1. Tell the students that they are going to act like detectives and solve several logic problems. Explain that they first need to identify the problem, and then look at the clues in order to solve the problems.
2. As an introduction to logic, place the *Back to School—One* transparency on the overhead.
3. Bring students' attention to the fact that there are three children and three ways to get to school. Ask the students what they think the problem is. [They need to figure out how each child gets to school.]

4. Direct their attention to the three clues. Read and discuss each clue and the information it provides. Demonstrate how to completely cover the grid with manipulatives and remove them based on the clues.
5. Distribute the *Back to School—Two* page to each student. Explain how to use the X and checkmark system, and allow time for them to solve the problem.
6. As appropriate throughout the year, distribute the different logic problems for students to work on.

Connecting Learning
1. How did you solve the problems?
2. Which clues were the most helpful? Why?
3. What kind of clues were confusing?
4. What does a sentence or clue with the word *not* tell you? If *not* tells you that something is not true, how might it also tell you something that is true?
5. What kinds of words told you to place an X (or remove a manipulative)?
6. If a clue gave you a direct yes, what did that tell you about the boxes above, below, and beside the yes response?

Solutions
Back to School—One
Monique rides to school in a car.
Juan must ride the bus because he does not walk (and Monique rides in a car).
Sadie must walk to school because she does not ride the bus (and Monique rides in a car).

Back to School—Two
Juan must ride the bus because he rides, but not in a car.
Sadie must ride in a car because Juan rides the bus and Sadie's best friend walks.
Monique must walk because Juan rides the bus and Sadie rides in a car.

A Logical Harvest
The yellow pumpkin must be last because it is not between other pumpkins and is not first.
The white pumpkin must be first because it is not between other pumpkins and yellow is last.
The orange and green pumpkins can't be first or last because they are *between* other pumpkins.
The orange pumpkin must be second because it is next to the white pumpkin, which is first.
The green pumpkin must be third because it is next to the yellow pumpkin, which is last.

Turkey Tracks
Pedro is the one with the fishing pole.
Tom must be the turkey tanning because Pedro likes to fish and Bob does not wear sunglasses.
Bob must be the one hiding because Pedro has a fishing pole and Tom is wearing sunglasses.

Winter Celebrations
Aman celebrates Kwanzaa.
Jacob must celebrate Chanukah because he lives next to Aman.
Lisa must celebrate Christmas because she can see a Menorah down the street.

Winter Wonderland
The winking snowflake is first.
The sad snowflake must be second because it is next to the winking snowflake.
The smiling snowflake must be third because it is next to the sad snowflake.
The surprised snowflake must be last.

Have a Heart
Maria had the most pink *Be Mine* hearts.
Abby had the most white *Kiss Me* hearts because the person with more white hearts is Maria's best friend and a girl.
Nick had the most purple *Love* hearts because he is a boy and Chen sits beside him.
Chen had the most green *Fax Me* hearts because Abby did not have many green.

Egg-cellent Logic
The spotted egg must be first because it is on the far left of the basket.
The chocolate egg must be second since it is between the spotted and striped eggs.
The striped egg must be third because it is next to the chocolate egg.
The egg with zigzags must be on the far right, or last, because it is not first, nor is it between other eggs.

Let's Go Fly a Kite
Cho must own the diamond-shaped kite because it has two tails.
Jose must own the fish kite because it reminds him of the ocean.
Sue must own the butterfly kite because Ali does not.
Ali must own the box kite.

* Reprinted with permission from *Principles and Standards for School Mathematics*, 2000 by the National Council of Teachers of Mathematics. All rights reserved.

Back to School—One

Monique, Sadie, and Juan come to school different ways.

1. Sadie does not ride the bus to school.
2. Juan likes to walk but does not walk to school.
3. Monique's mother drives her to school.

How does each person get to school?

Monique gets to school by _____.

Sadie gets to school by _____.

Juan gets to school by _____.

Back to School—Two

Monique, Sadie, and Juan come to school different ways.

1. Juan rides to school, but not in a car.
2. Sadie's best friend walks to school.

How does each person get to school?

Monique gets to school by _____.

Sadie gets to school by _____.

Juan gets to school by _____.

A Logical Harvest

One October morning a farmer discovered four colorful pumpkins growing in his garden. The yellow, orange, green, and white pumpkins grew in a row.

1. The yellow pumpkin was not first.
2. The orange pumpkin was between the green pumpkin and the white pumpkin.
3. The green pumpkin was between the yellow pumpkin and the orange pumpkin.

Color the pumpkins to show what the farmer saw.

Turkey Tracks

Tom, Bob, and Pedro live on a turkey farm.

1. Bob never wears sunglasses.
2. Pedro likes to fish.

Which turkey is which?

The fishing turkey is _____.

The tanning turkey is _____.

The hiding turkey is _____.

Winter Celebrations

Three families live beside each other. They each celebrate different winter holidays—Christmas, Chanukah, and Kwanzaa.

1. Jacob lives next to Aman.
2. Aman's house has Kwanzaa candles in the window.
3. Lisa can see a menorah in the window down the street.

Who celebrates each holiday?

Jacob celebrates _____.

Aman celebrates _____.

Lisa celebrates _____.

SOLVE IT! 2nd © 2005 AIMS Education Foundation

Winter Wonderland

One winter morning Mia looked out of her window and saw four beautiful snowflakes lined up from left to right on the windowsill.

1. The sad snowflake was between the winking snowflake and the smiling snowflake.
2. The first snowflake winked at Mia.

What order are the snowflakes in?

Have a Heart (Logic)

Four children sorted their candy hearts. Each had more of one kind than everyone else.

1. Abby did not have many green hearts.
2. The boy with the most *Love* hearts sits beside Chen.
3. The girl with more white hearts is Maria's best friend.
4. Maria had the most *Be Mine* hearts.

Who had more of each color heart?

Maria had more _____.   Nick had more _____.

Chen had more _____.   Abby had more _____.

Egg-cellent Logic

There are four eggs lined up in the basket from left to right.

1. The solid chocolate egg is between the striped egg and the spotted egg.
2. The zigzag egg is not first.
3. The spotted egg is on the far left of the basket.

How are the eggs lined up?

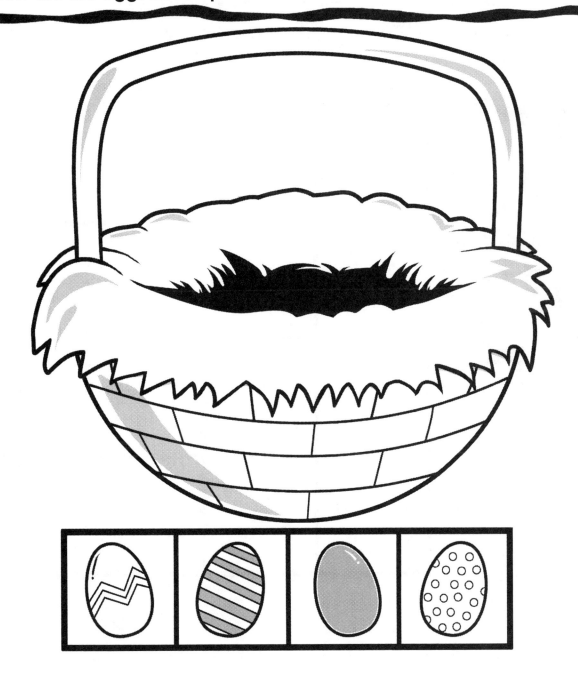

Let's Go Fly a Kite

Cho, Ali, Jose, and Sue each own a kite.

1. Ali loves butterflies but does not have a butterfly kite.
2. Jose's kite reminds him of the ocean.
3. Cho has a kite with two tails.

Who owns each kite?

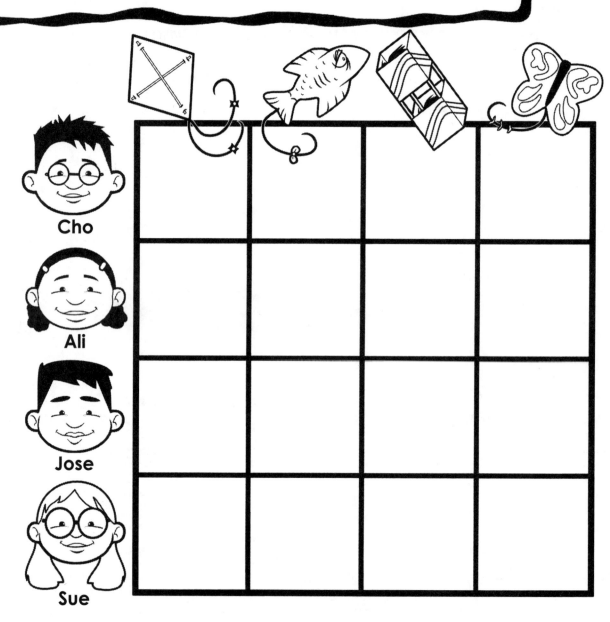

Cho's kite is _____.

Ali's kite is _____.

Jose's kite is _____.

Sue's kite is _____.

Arranging Astronauts

Topic
Logic

Key Question
How can you use clues to determine what order the astronauts are sitting in?

Learning Goal
Students will use logic clues to order a set of astronauts.

Guiding Document
NCTM Standards 2000*
- *Develop understanding of the relative position and magnitude of whole numbers and of ordinal and cardinal numbers and their connections*
- *Apply and adapt a variety of appropriate strategies to solve problems*
- *Build new mathematical knowledge through problem solving*

Math
Logic
Number sense
    ordinal numbers
Problem solving

Integrated Processes
Observing
Recording data
Organizing
Inferring
Applying

Problem-Solving Strategies
Use logical thinking
Use manipulatives
Organize the information

Materials
Astronaut counters in four colors
Crayons in colors to match the astronauts
Student pages

Background Information
For an adult, using logical thinking to make sense of simple clues and order objects is an easy task. For primary students, however, this skill must be learned. This activity provides an opportunity for young learners to practice logical thinking skills by using simple clues to order a set of either three or four astronauts. The clues will also give them practice identifying the ordinal numbers (first, second, third, etc.) and applying positional words (before, after, first, last, etc.).

Management
1. There are two levels of problems given—those that use three astronauts, and those that use four astronauts. Select the problems most appropriate for your students.
2. There are two student pages for each level of the problem. The first page for each level has both a picture of the shuttle with spaces for each astronaut and a traditional logic grid. Students can use whichever method is easiest to help them solve the problems. The second page has spaces for students to record their solutions. Depending on the number of problems you are doing, students may need more than one copy of the recording page. Alternately, you can have them create their own recording pages on scratch paper.
3. There are two approaches students can use to record their solutions in the logic grids. The easiest option is to have them place an astronaut (or make an X) in each box as it is eliminated as a possibility. The solution is then indicated by the empty boxes. The other option is simply the reverse of that. Students can begin with all of the squares covered with astronauts and remove astronauts as the clues eliminate certain possibilities. The solution in this case is indicated by the filled boxes.
4. Each student will need three or four colors of astronauts. The colors used in the clues are red, yellow, green, and blue.
5. Astronaut counters can be ordered from AIMS in packages of 100 (#1929), 300 (#1930), and 500 (#1931). If you do not have astronaut counters, you can copy the page of astronauts provided on different colors of paper or substitute other manipulatives in each color.

Procedure
1. Give each student a copy of the appropriate student pages and a few astronaut counters in each color. Explain that they will be putting the astronauts in order according to the clues you will be reading.
2. Discuss the different ways that students can go about solving each problem. They can place the astronauts

in spaces in the shuttle and move them around, or they can use the logic grid to eliminate options. If students are unfamiliar with logic grids, demonstrate how to use one by doing a sample problem.

3. Read the clues you selected aloud to the students. If appropriate, write the key portions of the clues on the board or overhead for students to refer to.

4. Re-read the clues several times so that students can check their answers. Once they are confident that they have the correct answer, ask them to color in the astronauts on the recording page to match their solutions.

5. After all of the clues have been read and solutions recorded, go back and have students share their solutions. Discuss the methods they used for arriving at those solutions, and address any discrepancies among the solutions.

Connecting Learning
1. How did you decide what order the astronauts should go in?
2. Was it easier for you to use the shuttle or the grid? Why?
3. How did having the astronauts help you solve the problems?
4. What would you have done if you hadn't had the astronauts?

Extensions
1. Create your own logic clues for students, or allow them to create clues for each other.
2. For advanced students, use more than four astronauts.

* Reprinted with permission from *Principles and Standards for School Mathematics*, 2000 by the National Council of Teachers of Mathematics. All rights reserved.

Arranging Astronauts Clues

Clues for three astronauts:
(blue, yellow, and red)

- The yellow astronaut is between the red and blue astronauts.
- The red astronaut is first.

- The red astronaut is not first.
- The blue astronaut is last.

- The blue astronaut is first.
- The yellow astronaut is before the red astronaut.

- The yellow astronaut is last.
- The red astronaut is after the blue astronaut.

- The blue astronaut is in the middle.
- The yellow astronaut is after the blue astronaut.

- The blue astronaut is not first.
- The red astronaut is after the blue astronaut.

Clues for four astronauts:
(blue, yellow, red, and green)

- The red and green astronauts are next to each other.
- The yellow astronaut is first.
- The green astronaut is last.

- The blue astronaut is after the yellow astronaut and before the green astronaut.
- The yellow astronaut is second.
- The red astronaut is not last.

- The green astronaut is third.
- The blue astronaut is before the red astronaut.
- The yellow astronaut is after the green astronaut.

- The yellow astronaut is before the red astronaut.
- The blue astronaut is second.
- The green astronaut is before the blue astronaut.

- The blue and green astronauts are next to each other.
- The yellow astronaut is next to the green astronaut.
- The red astronaut is last.
- The blue astronaut is not first.

ARRANGING ASTRONAUTS

	First	Second	Third
Red			
Yellow			
Blue			

SOLVE IT! 2nd © 2005 AIMS Education Foundation

ARRANGING ASTRONAUTS

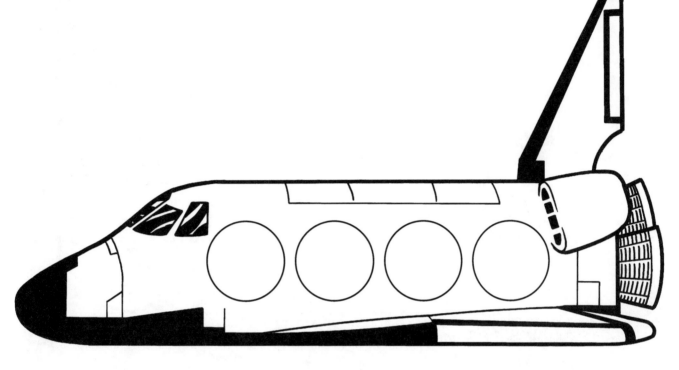

	First	Second	Third	Fourth
Red				
Yellow				
Green				
Blue				

Arranging Astronauts

Record your solutions.

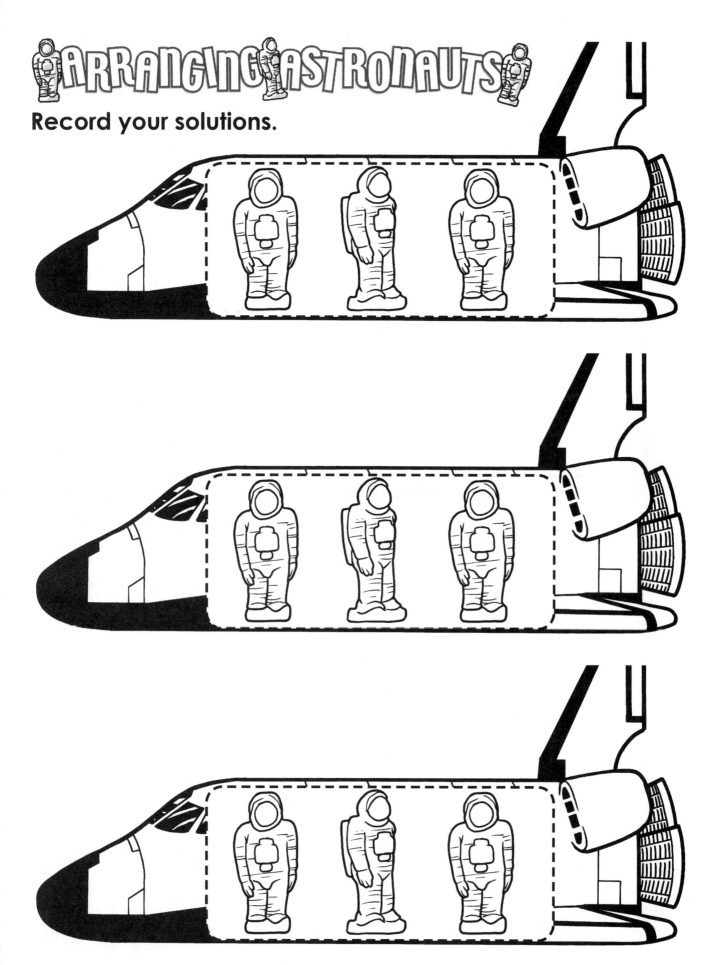

ARRANGING ASTRONAUTS

Record your solutions.

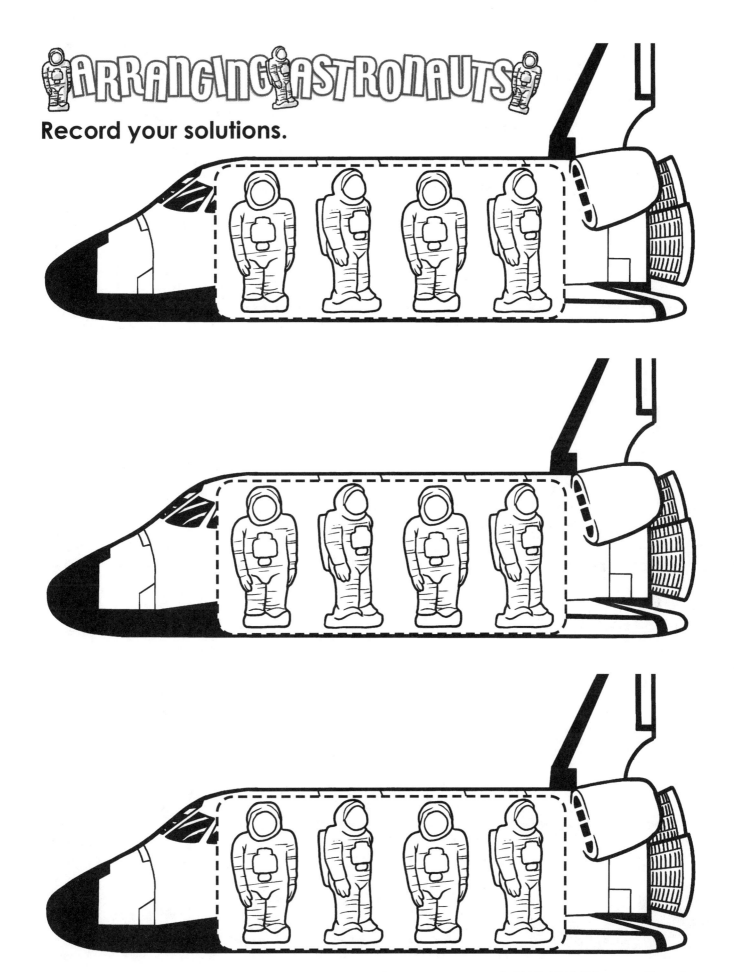

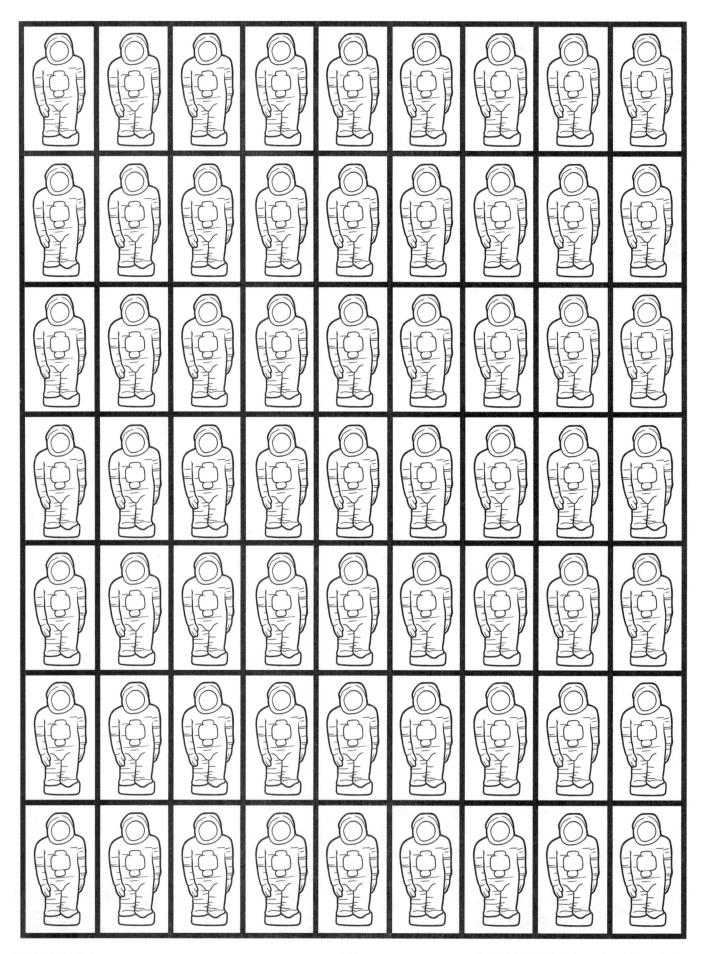

Teddy Bears on a Toboggan

Topic
Sequence logic

Key Question
In which order are the teddy bears riding on the toboggan?

Learning Goal
Students will use logical thinking skills to solve several problems.

Guiding Documents
Project 2061 Benchmarks
- *Some aspects of reasoning have fairly rigid rules for what makes sense; other aspects don't. If people have rules that always hold, and good information about a particular situation, then logic can help them to figure out what is true about it.*
- *Mathematical ideas can be represented concretely, graphically, and symbolically.*

NCTM Standards 2000*
- *Build new mathematical knowledge through problem solving*
- *Solve problems that arise in mathematics and in other contexts*
- *Apply and adapt a variety of appropriate strategies to solve problems*

Math
Logic
Sequencing
Problem solving

Integrated Processes
Observing
Organizing and recording data
Comparing and contrasting
Inferring
Drawing conclusions

Problem-Solving Strategies
Use logical thinking
Use manipulatives

Materials
For each pair of students:
4 Teddy Bear Counters (see *Management 1*)
crayons, markers, or colored pencils

For the teacher:
transparencies of activity pages
Friendly Bears, optional

Background Information
Logic problems have the potential of providing fun and a challenge for people of all ages, as well as providing opportunities to develop and reinforce logical thinking and problem-solving skills. Different people go about solving such problems in different ways. The explanation of the thought processes used to reach a conclusion is as significant as the conclusion itself. Occasionally there may be more than one reasonable answer to a problem, so it is important to consider the reasoning behind any alternate solutions that the students find.

Some students find it helpful to use manipulatives to solve logic problems. Others prefer using pencil and paper, or setting up a grid or similar format to work out a solution. Whatever process is used, students should test their conclusions against the clues, making adjustments until they are satisfied with the solutions they have found.

The puzzles in this collection are all *sequence* logic problems in which the challenge is to put the characters (in this case, colored bears) in order according to the clues. The following strategies may be helpful:

- If markers are used, begin by lining them up in random order; then keep rearranging them according to the clues until a solution is found.
- Read through all the clues before doing anything.
- Watch for hidden clues. For example, important information may be given in the first sentence(s) describing the puzzle situation, in addition to what is found in the clues themselves.
- Such terms as "immediately next to" and "right behind" indicate that no other bear is between the bears named.
- When a possible solution is found, go back and test every clue against it before recording.

Students may develop their own problem-solving strategies in addition to these suggestions.

SOLVE IT! 2nd © 2005 AIMS Education Foundation

Management
1. Each group will need Teddy Bear Counters in four colors: red, green, yellow, and blue. Other markers in these colors can be substituted if necessary.
2. Students who are not familiar with sequence logic problems will need to have some examples modeled. These could be demonstrated by naming three or four students and asking the class to put them in line according to such clues as "Robin is not the first person in line." or "The person with the red sweater is standing right between the person wearing glasses and the person wearing a white shirt."
3. Encourage the students to work in pairs and to talk about what they are thinking as they work on the problems.
4. Students work at different rates to solve logic puzzles. Tell those who reach a solution quickly to let you know in a subtle way so that they do not take away the excitement of solving a problem from those who are still working on it.
5. Some students may find it easier to use a grid format to solve the problems.

	1	2	3	4
Red				
Blue				
Yellow				
Green				

6. This set of problems is written so that each problem builds on the one before it. Those more experienced with solving logic problems will be able to solve the second and third puzzles using only the first two clues given if they notice that *all bears have changed position for each ride*. The fourth puzzle can only be solved using information from the first three.
7. If you wish to have students model their solutions on the overhead projector, you will need Friendly Bears or some other colored, translucent manipulative.

Procedure
1. If the students are familiar with sequence logic, go over the strategies, distribute the puzzle or puzzles, and let them work towards a solution.
2. If the students need more guidance, see *Management 1* and *2* for suggestions. You may wish to give them the activity page and read the clues out loud as they rearrange the markers and come to their own conclusions about each clue.
3. If you have Friendly Bears, ask different students to show their solutions using the overhead projector, explaining their thinking as they do so. Discuss the various strategies used.

Connecting Learning
1. Tell in your own words how you solved each puzzle. Did you solve each one the same way?
2. What clues were the most helpful to you? Explain.
3. How were the solutions and strategies used by other students similar to or different from yours?
4. If you were going to try some more of these puzzles, what would you do differently? What would you do the same way?
5. What advice would you give to someone who was about to try one of these puzzles for the first time?

Extension
Challenge the students to create their own sequence logic puzzles for their classmates to solve.

Solutions
Problem One
The order of the bears is red, blue, green, yellow.

Problem Two
The order of the bears is green, yellow, blue, red.

Problem Three
The order of the bears is blue, red, yellow, green.

Problem Four
The order of the bears is yellow, green, red, blue.

* Reprinted with permission from *Principles and Standards for School Mathematics*, 2000 by the National Council of Teachers of Mathematics. All rights reserved.

Teddy Bears on a Toboggan

Four teddy bears are having a wonderful time riding a toboggan down the hill together. Can you use these clues to find out the order they are seated on the toboggan?

1. The green bear is not sitting in the front seat.
2. One bear is sitting between the red bear and the green bear.
3. The yellow bear nearly got bounced out of the last seat on the way down the hill.

Color the bears to show your solution.

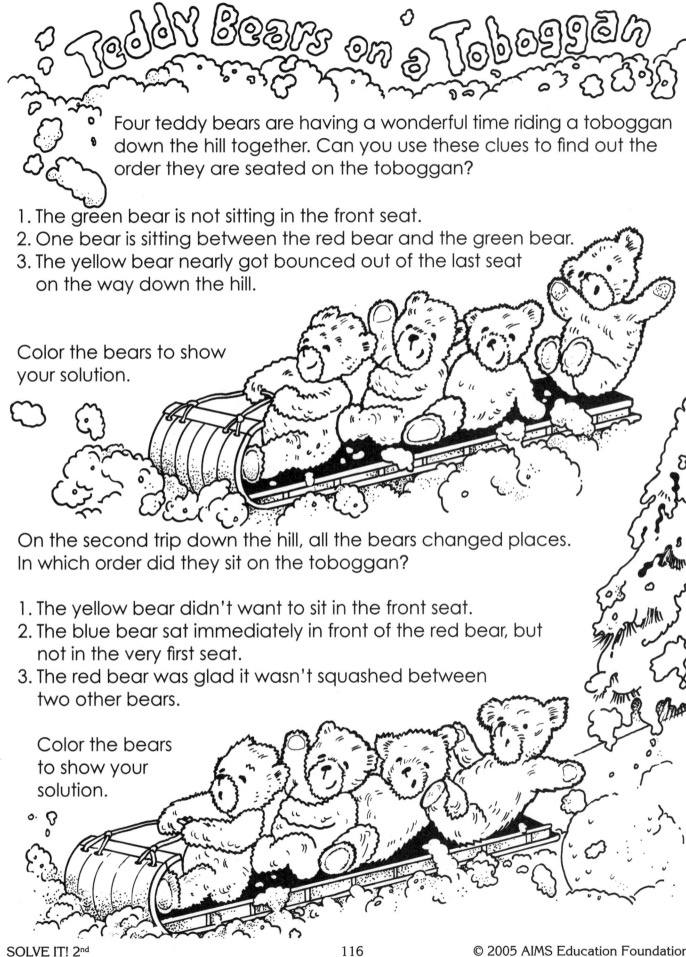

On the second trip down the hill, all the bears changed places. In which order did they sit on the toboggan?

1. The yellow bear didn't want to sit in the front seat.
2. The blue bear sat immediately in front of the red bear, but not in the very first seat.
3. The red bear was glad it wasn't squashed between two other bears.

Color the bears to show your solution.

On the third ride, the bears sat in a totally different order, with no bear sitting where it had sat before.

1. The green bear sat farther back than it had on either of the other rides.
2. The yellow bear still did not want to sit in the first seat.
3. The red bear sat right between the yellow bear and the blue bear.

Color the bears to show your solution.

On the fourth and final ride, every bear sat in a place where it had not sat before. Where did each bear sit?

Color the bears to show your solution.

Problem-Solving Strategies
Organize the Information

Graphs, tables, lists, and Venn diagrams are all organizational tools that are appropriate for young children. However, for organizing information to be relevant at the primary grades, there needs to be a purpose to organization. Students need to see that by organizing information they are organizing their thinking about the problem. This allows them to see what information they have and what is still needed to solve the problem.

Fishy Findings

Topic
Problem solving

Key Question
How many goldfish bowls will you need to buy so that all your fish will fit?

Learning Goal
Students will determine the number of small, medium, and large goldfish bowls that they need to buy in order for all of their goldfish to have a home.

Guiding Document
*NCTM Standards 2000**
- *Count with understanding and recognize "how many" in sets of objects*
- *Apply and adapt a variety of appropriate strategies to solve problems*
- *Solve problems that arise in mathematics and in other contexts*
- *Build new mathematical knowledge through problem solving*

Math
Number sense
   grouping
Problem solving

Integrated Processes
Observing
Collecting and recording data
Organizing data

Problem-Solving Strategies
Organize the information
Use manipulatives

Materials
Goldfish crackers
Goldfish "bowls" (see *Management 3*)
Student pages

Background Information
   For organizing information to be relevant at the primary grades, there needs to be a purpose to the organization. In this activity, students are challenged to find the number of bowls that need to be purchased to hold all of the goldfish that they have won at a carnival. Since they are too young to simply divide the number of fish by the number that will fit in each bowl, they need to have a way to organize the information so that they can come up with an answer. This is provided by giving them goldfish and bowls to manipulate, and then a way to record that information so that it can be used later.

Management
1. Each group will need goldfish crackers, fruit snack fish, or something about that size to represent fish.
2. The number of fish given to each group needs to be a multiple of two, three, and four (12, 24, 36, 48, etc.). Give each group the number of fish appropriate for their ability level. Different groups can have different numbers of fish.
3. Groups will need something to represent small, medium, and large fish bowls. Clear plastic cups in three sizes work well. You can also use plastic lids in three sizes (for example, yogurt, cottage cheese, and butter container lids). Each group will need multiple bowls of each size. (The number of bowls actually needed will depend on the number of fish, but groups should always have more bowls than they actually need so that the solution is not given away.)
4. The student pages have enough room to record up to 24 goldfish. If you give your students more than that, they will need to have multiple copies of each page.
5. This activity has the possibility for many extensions, and can be done at a variety of levels. Select the portions of the activity that are appropriate for your students.

Procedure
1. Have students get into groups and distribute the student pages and the appropriate number of goldfish and bowls to each group.
2. Tell students that they have won a bunch of goldfish at the carnival and need to buy bowls for all of them.
3. Explain that there are three sizes of bowls that they can buy—small, medium, and large. Only two fish will fit in each small bowl. Three fish will fit in each medium bowl, and four fish will fit in each large bowl.
4. Challenge students to determine how many bowls they would need to buy for their fish if they bought all small bowls, all medium bowls, or all large bowls.

SOLVE IT! 2nd   119   © 2005 AIMS Education Foundation

5. Instruct them to use the bowls and goldfish to organize the information. Once they have determined the total number of bowls necessary, have them record that information on the appropriate student page by drawing in the goldfish and writing the total number of bowls needed.
6. Discuss how students went about solving the problem and what solutions they got. If desired, repeat this process with more goldfish or move on to some of the extensions.

Connecting Learning
1. How many small goldfish bowls would your group need to buy? How did you get that answer?
2. How many medium goldfish bowls would your group need to buy? How did you get that answer?
3. How many large goldfish bowls would your group need to buy? How did you get that answer?
4. How could you have solved the problem without the goldfish and bowls?
5. How many bowls would you need if each bowl could hold six fish? How do you know?

Extensions
1. Make bar graphs of the number of small, medium, and large bowls that would need to be purchased for different numbers of fish.
2. Allow students to buy a combination of small, medium, and large bowls. Challenge them to see how many different combinations of small, medium, and large bowls they can use with their goldfish.
3. Assign prices to the different sizes of bowls and have students determine how much it would cost to buy enough bowls for their goldfish. Ask them to figure out which size of bowls would be the cheapest.
4. Change the number of fish that can fit in each bowl to include numbers that are not factors of the total number of fish (1, 5, 7, etc.). Challenge students to figure out the fewest possible number of bowls that could be purchased and the greatest possible number of bowls that could be purchased if each bowl had to be filled to capacity.

* Reprinted with permission from *Principles and Standards for School Mathematics*, 2000 by the National Council of Teachers of Mathematics. All rights reserved.

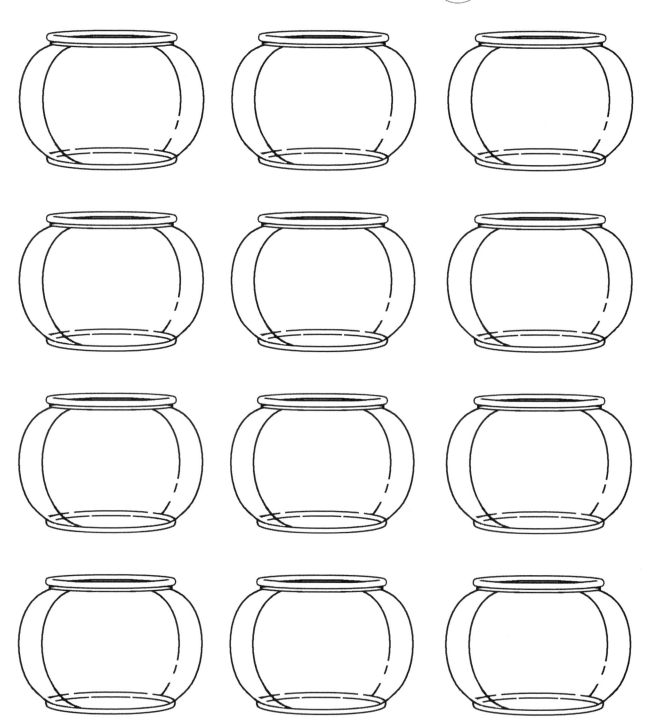

Fishy Findings

We have _____ fish.   We need _____ bowls.

SOLVE IT! 2nd 121 © 2005 AIMS Education Foundation

Fishy Findings

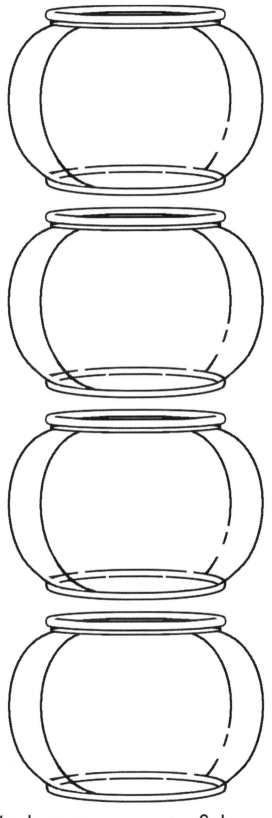
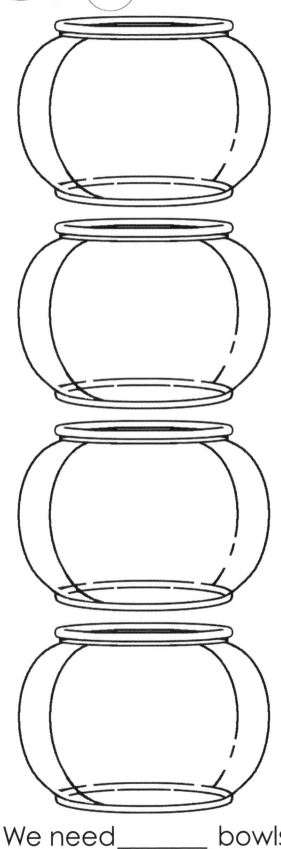

We have _____ fish.   We need _____ bowls.

SOLVE IT! 2ⁿᵈ   122   © 2005 AIMS Education Foundation

Fishy Findings

We have _____ fish.   We need _____ bowls.

SOLVE IT! 2ⁿᵈ   123   © 2005 AIMS Education Foundation

Playing with Probability

Topic
Probability

Key Question
How many rolls did it take you to finish the game?

Learning Goals
Students will:
1. play a game that involves rolling a die and moving a playing piece around the board,
2. keep track of how many rolls it takes each player to finish the game, and
3. compare these values to each other and the maximum and minimum possible number of rolls.

Guiding Document
NCTM Standards 2000*
- *Discuss events related to students' experiences as likely or unlikely*
- *Count with understanding and recognize "how many" in sets of objects*
- *Build new mathematical knowledge through problem solving*
- *Apply and adapt a variety of appropriate strategies to solve problems*

Math
Data collection
Counting
Probability
Estimation
Problem solving

Integrated Processes
Observing
Collecting and recording data
Comparing and contrasting
Generalizing

Problem-Solving Strategies
Organize the information
Use manipulatives

Materials
For each group:
 game board
 die
 game pieces (see *Management 1*)

For each student:
 student pages
 scratch paper

Background Information
The concept of probability is one that students are expected to begin learning at a very early age. The national reform documents include the study of basic probability as early as grades K-2, and many states have followed suit with their own standards. While a complete understanding of probability is not appropriate in the primary grades, foundational experiences that expose students to basic probability concepts are necessary for developing this understanding in later grades.

This activity also provides an ideal setting for students to exercise their problem-solving skills, as it gives them a meaningful context in which to organize information. The activity is designed as a game to be played in groups of two to four. The object of the game is for players to take turns rolling the die and moving their game pieces the corresponding number of spaces until they reach or exceed the *Finish* space. The emphasis is on keeping track of how many rolls it takes each player to do this and then to compare and contrast these values to each other, as well as to the maximum and minimum number of rolls possible.

Because there are 18 spaces on the game board (not including the *Start*), it is theoretically possible to move from the start to the finish in three rolls (by rolling a six each time); however, this is very unlikely. Likewise, it is possible, though extremely unlikely, that it could take a player 18 rolls to complete the journey (by rolling a one each time).

Management
1. Each group of students will need one copy of the game board, one die, and a game piece for each person. Teddy Bear Counters or other small manipulatives that come in multiple colors are ideal to use as game pieces. Groups should have no more than four students.
2. Each group will need two copies of the first student page and each student will need one copy of the final student page.
3. Copy the game boards onto card stock and laminate for extended use.

Procedure
1. Have students get into their groups and distribute the necessary materials for the game and scratch paper to each student.
2. Analyze the game as a class so that students are able to recognize and verbalize the "limits" to the number of rolls possible (see *Background*

SOLVE IT! 2ⁿᵈ

Information). Emphasize using the language of probability (likely, unlikely, certain, impossible, etc.). Use the questions provided to guide your discussion.

3. Instruct students to estimate how many rolls it will take them to finish their first games and write these numbers down on the scratch paper.
4. Instruct students to take turns rolling the die and moving their game pieces the appropriate number of spaces. For each roll of the die, they should make one tally mark on their scratch papers. No matter who finishes first, all players continue until they reach or exceed the *Finish* space.
5. Once a single round of play has been completed, take some time to discuss how the actual results compare to the estimates that students made.
6. Discuss what may have made some students over- or under-estimate the number of rolls it would take them to finish. Ask students to make new estimates as to how many rolls it will take them to finish next time.
7. Have students play another round and compare the estimates to the results once again. Play at least one more time after that so that students can begin to get an accurate sense of the average number of rolls it takes to finish the game.
8. Distribute two copies of the first student page to each group. Instruct them to work together to organize and record the information from all of their games. They should write each player's name, that player's estimate, and how many rolls it actually took that player to finish the game.
9. Once they have recorded the information from all of their games, distribute the final student page to each student and give them time to answer the questions using the information on the record pages.

Connecting Learning
Before you play:
1. What is the lowest number you can roll with a single die? [one]
2. What is the highest number you can roll with a single die? [six]
3. Are you more likely, less likely, or equally likely to roll a one or a six? …a four or a five? …a two or a three, etc.? [There is an equal chance of rolling every number on a die.]
4. How many spaces are there on the game board? [18, not including the start]
5. What is the fewest number of rolls it could take to win? [three]
6. What would you have to roll in order to win this quickly? [all sixes]
7. Do you think this is likely to happen, or unlikely? [unlikely] Why? [You don't often roll the same thing three times in a row.]
8. What is the greatest number of rolls it could take to win? [18]
9. What would you have to roll in order for it to take this many rolls? [all ones]

10. Do you think this is likely to happen, or unlikely? [very unlikely] Why? [You would have to roll a one 18 times in a row.]

After playing one game:
1. How many rolls did it actually take you to win?
2. Is this number greater than what you estimated, less than what you estimated, or exactly what you estimated? Why?
3. How many rolls did it take your partners to win?
4. If you were to play another round, do you think it would take more, fewer, or the same number of rolls for you to win? Why?

After playing two games:
1. How many rolls did it take for you to win this time?
2. Is this number greater than what you estimated, less than what you estimated, or exactly what you estimated?
3. Was it easier to estimate how many rolls it would take you to win this time? [Hopefully, yes.] Why or why not? [After having played once, students should have a better idea of the average number of rolls it takes to win.]
4. Was the number of rolls it took you to win the same as or different from the first time you played? (If it was different) Why do you think it was different?

After playing three or more games:
1. Think about how many rolls it took you to win each time and how many rolls it took your partners to win each time. Can you say about how many rolls it "usually" takes to win?
2. How does this number compare to your first guess? …your second guess?
3. Can you make a probability statement about the number of rolls it takes to finish the game? [It is likely that I can finish the game in six rolls. It is unlikely that I can finish the game in three rolls. It is unlikely that it would take 10 rolls to finish the game.]
4. How did organizing the information help you to answer these questions?

Extensions
1. Compile each group's data from all games to determine a class average for how many rolls it takes to finish.
2. Change the number of spaces on the game board and see how the results compare.

* Reprinted with permission from *Principles and Standards for School Mathematics*, 2000 by the National Council of Teachers of Mathematics. All rights reserved.

Playing with Probability

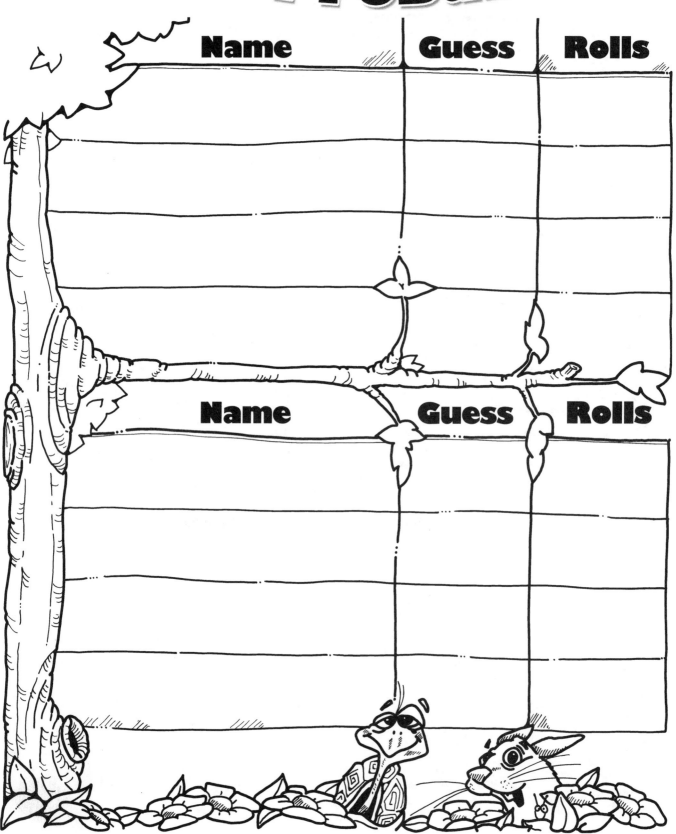

Organize your information to answer these questions:

1. How many rolls does it "usually" take to win?

2. How does this number compare to your first guess? How does it compare to your second guess?

3. Use the information to make a probability statement about the number of rolls it takes to finish the game.

Sign-in Sheets and Data Displays

Topic
Data analysis

Key Question
How can we show the results of a survey?

Learning Goals
Students will:
1. represent data using tables and graphs, and
2. compare different representations of the same data.

Guiding Documents
Project 2061 Benchmark
- Simple graphs can help to tell about observations.

NRC Standards
- Use data to construct a reasonable explanation.
- Communicate investigations and explanations.

NCTM Standards 2000*
- Pose questions and gather data about themselves and their surroundings
- Represent data using concrete objects, pictures, and graphs
- Describe parts of the data and the set of data as a whole to determine what the data show
- Build new mathematical knowledge through problem solving

Math
Data analysis
Graphing
Problem solving

Integrated Processes
Observing
Classifying
Comparing and contrasting
Collecting and recording data
Interpreting data
Communicating
Inferring

Problem-Solving Strategy
Organize the information

Materials
For each group:
chart paper
markers
3 ring binder or spiral notebook for sign in questions

For the class:
overhead transparencies (see *Management 7*)

Background Information
This activity is designed to encourage students to communicate information gleaned from survey questions. The survey questions will be collected in a book that students sign daily with their responses. When ample questions and responses have been gathered, each student group will be given one question. Students will then use their problem-solving skills to create data displays and write statements to communicate the results.

Management
1. This activity is not designed to be a preliminary experience with data organization. It should follow several experiences in which the children have built various graphs and discussed data displays. Students should already be able to use appropriate labels on various tables and data display models.
2. Data for this activity are collected over several weeks. Each day there will be a different question for students to respond to in the sign-in book. After two weeks, there should be enough question pages for each group to have one. Simply remove the completed pages and distribute one page to each group. The group will decide how best to display the data and describe the results.
3. Questions for the sign-in book should be easily answered. Did you do your homework *after school, after dinner,* or *this morning?* What time did you get up this morning? What color is your favorite fruit? etc.
4. This activity works best in groups of four.
5. The data display and interpretation will take place over several days.
6. Chart paper with grid lines may be helpful for graphic display.

SOLVE IT! 2nd   129   © 2005 AIMS Education Foundation

7. Make a transparency of one of the sign-in sheets generated by the students and the page of sample data organizers.
8. Make several copies of the conversation bubble page for interpreting the information.

Procedure
Part One
1. Tell the students that they will be constructing a data display for one of the questions from the sign-in book.
2. Place the transparency of one page from the sign-in book on the overhead. Discuss the information gathered.
3. Place the transparency of the sample data organizers on the overhead and discuss how to best display the data from this sign-in sheet. Together, make a graph or table of the data.
4. Invite students to look at the data display and give true statements about data. Record several of the statements in the conversation bubbles and place them around the graph or table. Explain that you are using the conversation bubbles to tell the story of the data.

Part Two
1. Review the graph (or table) made in *Part One*.
2. Give one page from the sign-in book and a copy of the page of sample data organizers to each group.
3. Distribute chart paper and markers to be used for construction of the data table or graph.
4. Allow time for groups to discuss their data and construct an appropriate data display. They can use words and/or pictures as appropriate.
5. When all groups have completed a data display for their questions, collect them for future use.

Part Three
1. Review the true statements recorded in the conversation bubbles in *Part One*.
2. Tell the students that they will be interpreting the graphs that were made from their sign-in data.
3. Distribute the data displays from *Part Two* and several conversation bubbles to each group and allow time for interpretation. Give each group a data display that they did not construct. Have groups record true statements about the data in the conversation bubbles.
4. When all groups have recorded their responses, gather the students together, and have each group share the data and their interpretations.
5. Allow time for questions and comments about the data displays and the stories of the data.

Connecting Learning
1. How did you represent your data?
2. What conclusions did you draw from your data?
3. What strategy did your group use to decide which graph or table would be the best to show your data?
4. If you asked the same question in another classroom, do you think the results would be the same? Why or why not?
5. Were there any questions that had different results than you thought they would have? Why?
6. Is there another way you could have shown your data? Would that have made it easier to interpret? Why or why not?
7. What did you learn about representing data by doing this activity?
8. What is a question you would like to ask in our sign-in book?

Extensions
1. Continue to have students sign in throughout the year and repeat the activity using other questions and other data display methods.
2. Have the students take a sign-in question home for someone to answer. Display the results of the home sign-in data.

* Reprinted with permission from *Principles and Standards for School Mathematics,* 2000 by the National Council of Teachers of Mathematics. All rights reserved.

Sign-in Sheets and Data Displays
Sample Data Organizers

Number of leaves collected

Maple	3
Birch	5
Oak	1

Table

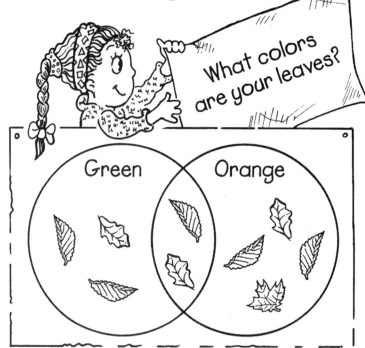

Venn Diagram

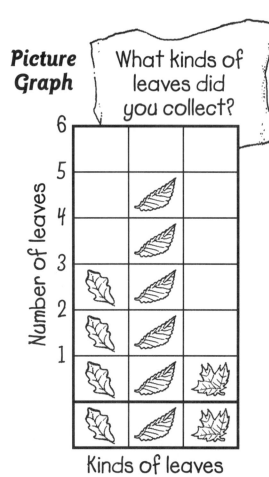

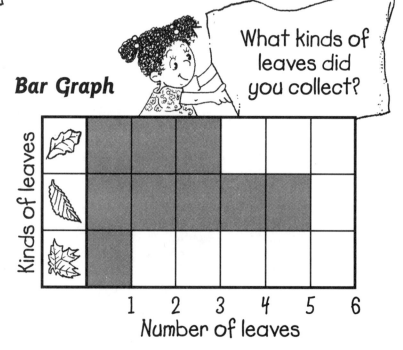

SOLVE IT! 2nd — 131 — © 2005 AIMS Education Foundation

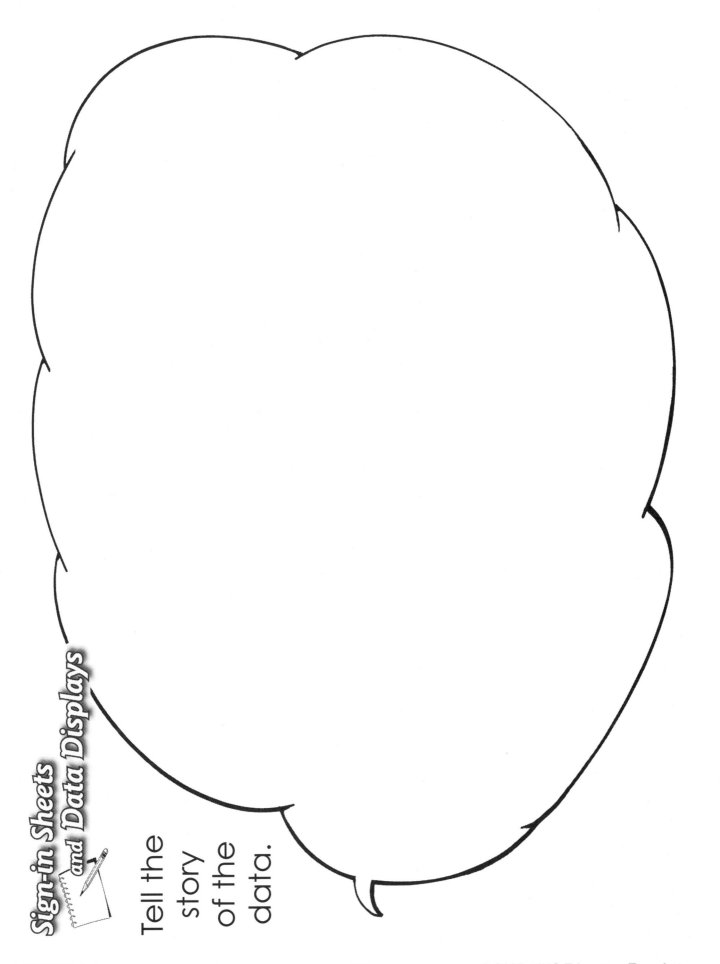

Sign-in Sheets and Data Displays

Tell the story of the data.

Problem-Solving Strategies: Work Backwards

The problem-solving strategy of working backwards is simply taking a regular problem and doing it in reverse. This strategy is appropriate to use when the goal or final destination is known, but there is a variety of ways to get to that goal or destination. In problems like these, working backwards allows you to determine the best steps to take. It is also appropriate to work backwards when you know the end result or answer and need to determine the starting point. For example, if you want to know how much money you started with at the beginning of the week, and you know how much money you ended with and all of the transactions you made during the week, you can work backwards to figure out the starting amount.

Counting Back Answers

Topic
Problem solving

Key Question
How can we begin with the end result, analyze each step, and figure what we started with?

Learning Goal
Students will determine the number of objects they started with based on how many they gave away and how many they have left.

Guiding Document
NCTM Standards 2000*
- *Develop a sense of whole numbers and represent and use them in flexible ways including relating, composing, and decomposing numbers*
- *Count with understanding and recognize "how many" in sets of objects*
- *Apply and adapt a variety of appropriate strategies to solve problems*
- *Build new mathematical knowledge through problem solving*
- *Solve problems that arise in mathematics and in other contexts*

Math
Number and operations
 addition
 subtraction
Problem solving

Integrated Processes
Observing
Comparing and contrasting
Collecting and recording data
Interpreting data

Problem-Solving Strategies
Work backwards
Use manipulatives

Materials
Container (see *Management 1*)
A collection of objects (see *Management 2*)

Background Information
The problem-solving strategy of working backwards is simply taking a regular problem and doing it in reverse. It is appropriate to work backwards when you know the end result or answer and need to determine the starting point. In this activity, students will build an understanding of how this strategy works by physically retracing their steps and then will have an opportunity to practice using the strategy in problems similar to ones they might actually encounter in life and on standardized tests.

Management
1. The first scenario suggests a basket; however, any container will work.
2. The objects suggested for the scenarios are apples, erasers, pencils and money; however, other math manipulatives such as Unifix cubes would also work.

Procedure
1. Gather the class around a basket containing two apples.
2. Tell the class that you would like them to help you solve a problem. Explain that earlier in the day you had several apples in the basket and that now you only have two apples in the basket. Tell the class you also gave some apples to different people during the day and you now need to know how many apples you started with. Allow the class to brainstorm possible ways to solve the problem.
3. If no one suggests working backwards to solve the problem, ask the class if they have ever lost something and retraced their steps to find it. Suggest that they help you retrace your steps to solve the problem.
4. Tell the class that you met the principal in the lunchroom and gave him an apple for dessert and that you also gave two apples to the secretary early this morning. Write *principal—one apple* and *secretary—two apples* on the board.
5. Invite three students to assist you as you retrace your steps. One student will represent you and will hold the basket containing two apples. Another student will represent the principal and should have one apple. A third student will represent the secretary and should have two apples.

SOLVE IT! 2nd 134 © 2005 AIMS Education Foundation

6. Ask the person representing you to stand at the front of the room with the basket and position the "principal" and "secretary" at two different locations in the room. Instruct the student representing you to retrace your steps and collect the apples to see how many were in the basket to start with.
7. Discuss how working backwards helped you solve your problem.
8. Write the following problems on the board and ask the class to help you solve them by working backwards.
   - Diego gave two erasers to his friend Kim. He gave three to his teacher and he has five left. How many erasers did Diego start with?
   - Bobby has 10 cents. He spent five cents on an eraser and 10 cents on a pencil. How much money did he start with?
   - I gave three pencils to a friend, lost five on the way to school and broke two. I have six pencils left. How many pencils did I start with?

Connecting Learning
1. How did you figure out the answers to the questions?
2. How did retracing your steps help you better understand the working backwards strategy?
3. Would you have been able to solve any of the problems without working backwards? Why or why not?
4. Was it easier to work the problems out in your head or to physically retrace your steps? Why?
5. Can you think of other times when you would use the strategy of working backwards?

Extensions
1. Use the working backwards strategy to solve various questions using a calendar. For example, if my birthday is January 15th and my party will be three days before my birthday, what day will my birthday party be?
2. Use the book *Alexander, Who Used to Be Rich Last Sunday* by Judith Viorst. Start by discussing how much money he has at the end of the book, list all of his expenditures, and ask the class to figure out how much he started with.

* Reprinted with permission from *Principles and Standards for School Mathematics*, 2000 by the National Council of Teachers of Mathematics. All rights reserved.

Turning Back Time

Topic
Problem solving

Key Question
How can we decide when to begin a task if we know how long the task will take and when it must be finished?

Learning Goals
Students will:
1. use paper plates representing durations of time to determine when to begin a task given the ending time, and
2. use model watches to determine when to begin a task given an ending time.

Guiding Document
*NCTM Standards 2000**
- *Recognize the attributes of length, volume, weight, area, and time*
- *Understand how to measure using nonstandard and standard units*
- *Use tools to measure*
- *Build new mathematical knowledge through problem solving*
- *Solve problems that arise in mathematics and in other contexts*

Math
Measurement
    time
Problem solving

Integrated Processes
Observing
Comparing and contrasting
Applying
Relating

Problem-Solving Strategies
Work backwards
Use manipulatives

Materials
For the class:
    paper plates (see *Management 1*)
    event cards
    wristwatch transparency (see *Management 4*)
    card stock

For each student:
    student watches (see *Management 2*)
    two cotter pins (see *Management 6*)

Background Information
The problem-solving strategy of working backwards is one that we often use in our everyday lives. For example, if you have to be at work at 8:00 and it takes you 30 minutes to drive there and one hour to get ready, you know you need to get up at 6:30 to be on time. Often children use this strategy when they want to watch a particular television show at a certain time and they have homework and chores to do.

In this activity, students will choose an event and identify the time the event takes place. They will then be given information about tasks to complete and how long those take. From this, they will work backwards to determine the time they should begin to get to the event on time.

Management
1. Gather several paper plates. Cut some of the plates in half to represent half-hours and leave the others whole to represent whole hours.
2. Prior to this lesson, make copies of the watches on cardstock—enough for one per student—and laminate for durability.
3. Copy one set of event cards onto card stock and cut them apart.
4. When first introducing the concept of working backwards using time, it is suggested that you use only full hours and then progress to a combination of hours and half-hours as students show an understanding of the process.
5. Make a transparency of one of the student wristwatches and attach the cotter pins as illustrated.

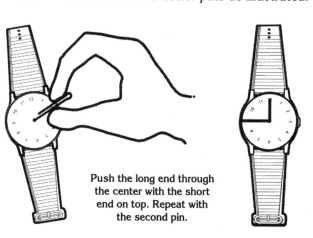

Push the long end through the center with the short end on top. Repeat with the second pin.

SOLVE IT! 2nd © 2005 AIMS Education Foundation

6. Cotter pins can be purchased at most local hardware stores. They are similar to bobby pins, but come in a variety of lengths. Each watch will need two cotter pins—one $\frac{3"}{32} \times \frac{3"}{4}$ and one $\frac{3"}{32} \times \frac{1"}{2}$. Students will need assistance punching a hole in the center of the watch and pushing in the two pins.
7. Since it is difficult to move the smaller hour hand over the top of the larger minute hand (or vice versa), you will need to be careful that the times you select in *Part Two* do not cause this to happen.

Procedure
Part One
1. Ask the *Key Question*. Discuss the reasonableness of the responses.
2. Display the birthday invitation event card so that the students can see it. Tell the class that you have been invited to a party at 2:00 on Saturday. Explain that you have several things to do before the party. Ask them to help you decide when you should leave home so that you get to the party on time.
3. Show the class a whole paper plate and tell them that you would like to use it to represent things that take an hour to do. Discuss why a whole paper plate might be a good representation of an hour. [It is one whole object; when making paper plate clocks, the minute hand goes all the way around the clock every 60 minutes or hour.]
4. Display one of the half plates and ask the class what they think the half plate will represent. [half-hours]
5. Bring student's attention back to the 2:00 party and explain that it will take you one hour to purchase a gift and get it wrapped at the mall. As you say this, place a whole paper plate to the left of the 2:00 party invitation.
6. Ask the class what time you would have to leave home in order to be on time for the party if you have no other errands. [1:00]
7. Tell the class that you also have to visit a sick friend on Saturday and that it will take about two hours. As you say this, place two additional whole paper plates to the left of the first plate. Ask the class to help you figure out what time you will need to leave home in order to get to the party at 2:00. Guide students by starting at the party and working back one hour at a time to determine the time that you should leave home. Discuss how it would have been different if you had errands that would have taken a half hour instead of an hour. Challenge the class to use the additional event cards and the work backwards strategy to solve the problems.

T.V. scenario—Your favorite television show comes on at 5:00. You have half an hour's worth of chores to do, half an hour of homework, and a one-hour piano lesson. What time will you have to start so that you will be finished by 5:00 when your show comes on?

Bedtime scenario—Your bedtime is 8:30. If you want to hear a bedtime story, it will take 30 minutes. Your bath will take half an hour. Dinner will take an hour. What time will you need to eat so that you will be ready for bed at 8:30?

School ends scenario—School ends at 3:00. There is one hour of math, one hour of reading, one hour of science, one hour of physical education, and half an hour for lunch. What time does school start?

School scenario—School starts at 8:00. It takes you one hour to eat, brush your teeth, and get dressed. It takes half an hour to drive to school. What time do you have to get up?

Soccer game scenario—The game starts at 4:30. You have to pick up the team. That will take one hour. You also need to pick up snacks for the team. That will take half an hour. What time do you have to leave home?

Part Two
1. Distribute the watches and assist students with the attachment of the cotter pins.
2. Explain to the class that they will be solving several problems similar to the problems in the previous experience. However, this time they will be using their paper wristwatches instead of paper plates.
3. Display the wristwatch transparency. Set your watch to show 12:00. Instruct the class to do the same. Ask the class what time it was one hour ago. Encourage students to share the strategies they used to determine the new time. Demonstrate how they can move the hour hand back from the 12 to the 11 if they want to go back one hour in time.
4. Tell the students to again set their watches to 12:00. Ask them what time it was three hours ago. Continue this process until all students are confident that they can go back in time when given on-the-hour times.

5. Repeat procedures 3 and 4 starting at 12:30. Continue this process until all students are confident that they can go back in time when given on-the-half hour times.
6. Repeat procedures 3 and 4 using a combination of hours and half hours.
7. When students are comfortable using their watches to work backwards, challenge them to use their wristwatches to solve the following problems:
   - Your dance lesson starts at 4:30. If it takes you one hour to get to the dance studio, when do you have to leave?
   - Your plane leaves at 9:30. You have to get to the airport two hours before your departure time. It takes you half an hour to get to the airport. What time do you have to leave home?
   - Your class returned from the zoo fieldtrip at 3:30. You spent one hour visiting the mammals, one hour visiting the reptiles, and half an hour driving to the zoo. What time did the fieldtrip begin?
   - The bake sale starts at 4:00. It will take you an hour to bake brownies and half an hour to drive to the sale. When do you have to start the brownies?
8. Discuss the problem-solving strategies used by the students.

Connecting Learning
1. How did you figure out the answers to each question?
2. How did using paper plates to represent hours and a half-hours help you better understand the working backwards strategy?
3. Would you have been able to solve any of the problems without working backwards? Why or why not?
4. Was it easier to work the problems out in your head or to physically move the hands of the clock? Why?
5. Why is it important to know how long an event takes and how much time you have?

* Reprinted with permission from *Principles and Standards for School Mathematics*, 2000 by the National Council of Teachers of Mathematics. All rights reserved.

Turning Back Time

2:00 Birthday Party

5:00 Favorite TV Show

Turning Back Time

8:30
Bed Time

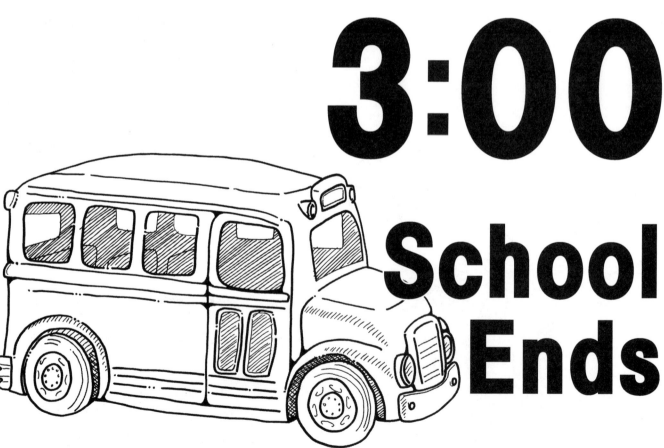

3:00
School Ends

Turning Back Time

8:00 School Starts

4:30 Soccer Game

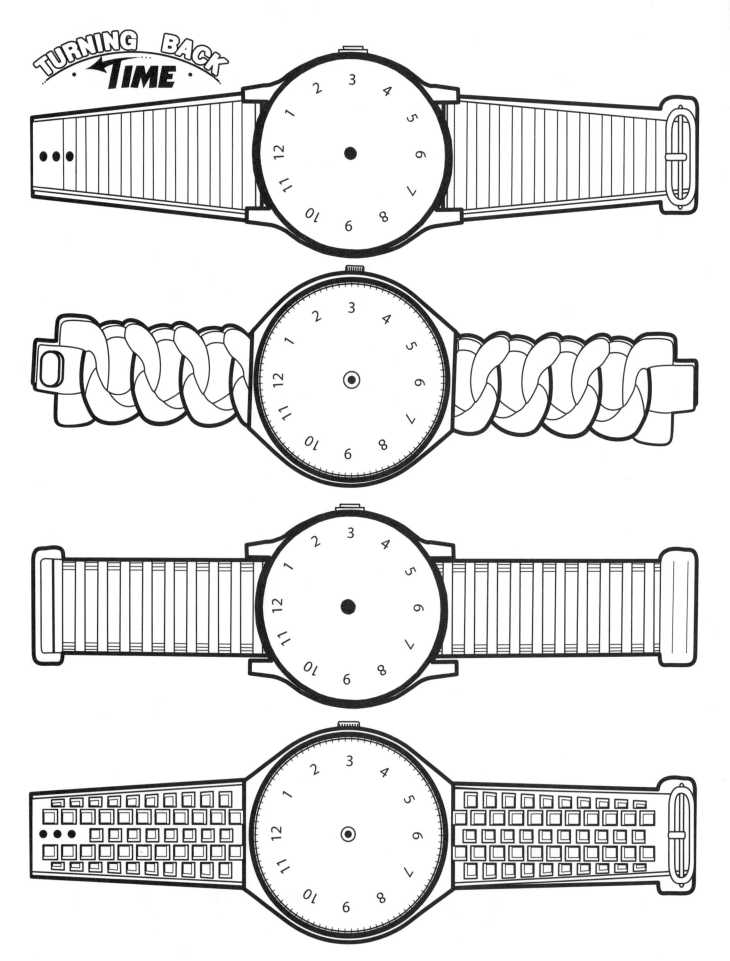

Change Confusion

Topic
Problem solving

Key Question
How can you figure out the amount of change you should receive when buying something?

Learning Goals
Students will:
1. determine the amount of change they should have received based on how much they spent and what they bought, and
2. find the person in their group who got the amount of change they should have.

Guiding Document
NCTM Standards 2000*
- *Develop a sense of whole numbers and represent and use them in flexible ways including relating, composing, and decomposing numbers*
- *Count with understanding and recognize "how many" in sets of objects*
- *Apply and adapt a variety of appropriate strategies to solve problems*
- *Solve problems that arise in mathematics and in other contexts*
- *Build new mathematical knowledge through problem solving*

Math
Whole number operations
    addition
    subtraction
Problem solving

Integrated Processes
Observing
Comparing and contrasting
Inferring

Problem-Solving Strategies
Work backwards
Use manipulatives

Materials
Play money (see *Management 7*)
Envelopes
Card sets
Menu page

Background Information
The strategy of working backwards is one that we are often called on to use in our everyday lives. In this activity, students are given the opportunity to practice using this strategy in a setting similar to one they might actually encounter. They are customers in an ice cream shop where the clerk is a little careless. They know what they purchased and how much money they gave the clerk, but the amount of change is incorrect. They must figure out the amount of change that should have been received and identify the person within their group who received that amount.

Management
1. There are eight sets of cards that can be used in groups of four. The cards vary in difficulty based on the cost of the item purchased. This allows you to differentiate the problem for students at different skill levels.
2. The card sets need to be cut out and placed in envelopes for students ahead of time. It is very important that cards from one set stay together or there will not be the correct change for everyone in the group. Sets are identified by the letter in the upper left corner of the card.
3. Each card shows what was purchased, what was given to the clerk, and what was received in change. Ideally, the section showing the change should be cut off and replaced with play money. If you don't have play money, simply cut the two sections apart so that students can match the correct change with the correct card.
4. All students will need to know the menu prices. You can make an overhead transparency of the menu page, make a large poster of the prices, write the prices on the chalkboard, or give each group its own copy of the menu page.
5. This activity assumes a familiarity with coins and their values and an understanding of how to make change.
6. If desired, this activity can be acted out as a whole-class role play, with you as the careless store clerk and the students as the customers.
7. If using play money, you will need 25 nickels, 28 dimes, and 13 quarters.

Procedure
1. Have students get into groups of four and give each group a set of envelopes with problems appropriate for their ability levels.

2. Explain that they are going to be pretending to be customers in an ice cream shop where the clerk is a little careless. He often makes mistakes when giving back change. They must carefully check his math to see if they got the right amount of money back. If they didn't, they must see if someone else in their group got the amount they should have received and trade their change.
3. Have each student open his or her envelope and look at what was purchased. Display the menu or give each group a copy of the page.
4. Have students look at the amount of change they were given and determine if they got the correct amount. If they didn't, have them find the person in their group who got the change they should have.
5. When all groups have determined the correct amount of change for each purchase, check to make sure that they are correct. Talk about the process students went through to correctly distribute the change.
6. Discuss how much they received in change, how much they should have received, which was more or less, etc.
7. Repeat this process as many times as desired, giving different groups different sets of problems.

Connecting Learning
1. What did you buy?
2. How much did it cost?
3. How much money did you give the clerk?
4. How much did you get in change?
5. What should you have received in change?
6. Did you receive more or less than you should have? How much more (or less)?
7. Why is it important to know how to count money?

* Reprinted with permission from *Principles and Standards for School Mathematics*, 2000 by the National Council of Teachers of Mathematics. All rights reserved.

F

F

F

F

F

F

F

F

SOLVE IT! 2nd   151   © 2005 AIMS Education Foundation

SOLVE IT! 2nd 153 © 2005 AIMS Education Foundation

Trip Trackers

Topic
Problem solving

Key Question
How can you figure out the route by looking at a map and listening to clues?

Learning Goal
Students will work backwards to identify routes described by studying the map.

Guiding Document
NCTM Standards 2000*
- *Describe, name, and interpret relative positions in space and apply ideas about relative position*
- *Describe, name, and interpret direction and distance in navigating space and apply ideas about direction and distance*
- *Find and name locations with simple relationships such as "near to" and in coordinate systems such as maps*
- *Apply and adapt a variety of appropriate strategies to solve problems*
- *Build new mathematical knowledge through problem solving*
- *Solve problems that arise in mathematics and in other contexts*

Math
Geometry
   spatial relationships
Problem solving

Integrated Processes
Observing
Comparing and contrasting
Applying

Problem-Solving Strategies
Work backwards
Draw out the problem

Materials
Map pages
Dry erase markers (see *Management 4*)

Background Information
   The context of a map with clearly identified locations is one that presents many opportunities for young learners. In this activity, the map is used to reinforce the geometric skills of spatial relationships while working on the problem-solving skill of working backwards.

   Students are given scenarios describing paths that people take from one location to another. They use the map to work backwards to determine the path that generated the results described.

Management
1. Students can work on this activity individually or in pairs.
2. To do this activity, students will need to be familiar with the directional words *north*, *south*, *east*, and *west* and know how to apply them on a map.
3. Copy the map pages onto card stock and laminate. If you wish to have students color the maps, do that the day before presenting the activity.
4. Provide students with dry erase markers, overhead pens, or wax pencils so they can show the routes for each problem and then erase them.

Procedure
1. Give each student (or pair) a copy of the first map page. Tell them to orient it so that north is at the top of the page. If necessary, review the four directions and how to use them to locate things on a map.
2. Read the first set of scenarios aloud to the class. You may also wish to write the key components of the scenarios on the board for students to reference.
3. Clarify that in order for a route to "pass" or "go by" a location, the route must go in front of or alongside the location mentioned. Passing by the corner only doesn't count.
4. For each scenario, have students draw the route and use words to describe the route. For instance, "Go north on Main Street, then east on Third."
5. Repeat this process for the second map and its scenarios.

Connecting Learning
1. What problem-solving strategy did you use to solve the problems?
2. How did having the map help you?
3. Are there other times when you would want to use a similar strategy to solve a problem?

Extensions
1. Add locations and/or houses to the map to increase difficulty.
2. Have students create their own problems to go along with the maps.

* Reprinted with permission from *Principles and Standards for School Mathematics*, 2000 by the National Council of Teachers of Mathematics. All rights reserved.

Trip Trackers

Map One Problems
1. Mandy walks to the library on Saturday mornings. She does not walk by the playground. What is the shortest route she can take?
2. Tyra walks to school every morning. She does not walk by Chen's house. She does not walk by Mandy's house. How does she get to school?
3. Chen likes to walk to Zack's house. To get there, he passes by the park. He does not go by the grocery store or the school. How does he get there?
4. Diego likes to take a long walk home from school. First he goes by the playground. Then he walks by the library. Next he passes Tyra's house. Then he goes by Chen's house. How does he get home?
5. Zack walked home from the museum. He passed Tyra, Chen, Diego, and Mandy's houses. He also passed the grocery store and the park. He did not pass the school. How did he walk?
6. Mandy's mom works at the museum. After work, she dropped a book off at the library, picked up Mandy from school, went by the grocery store, and went home. What route did she take?
7. On the way to school, Diego likes to walk so that he doesn't pass the houses of any of his friends (Tyra, Chen, Mandy, and Zack). What is the shortest way he can get to school?

Solutions to Map One Problems*
1. Mandy walks south on Main Street and east on First to get to the library.
2. Tyra walks east on First and north on American to get to school.
3. Chen walks north on Lake Drive to Fourth, walks northeast on Fourth to Main Street, and north on Main Street to get to Zack's house.
4. Diego goes south on American to First. He goes west on First to Lake Drive. He goes north on Lake Drive to Second to get home.
5. Zack walked east on First to Lake Drive. He walked north on Lake Drive to Third. He walked east on Third to Main Street. He walked north on Main Street to get home.
6. Mandy's mom drove east on First to American (stopping at the library). She went north on American to Third (stopping at the school). She went east on Third to Main to get home (stopping at the grocery store).
7. Diego walks east on Second to Lake Drive, where he turns north. He walks north on Lake Drive to Fourth. He goes northeast on Fourth to Main Street. He heads south on Main Street to Third. He walks east on Third to the school.

Map Two Problems
1. Zack walks to Tyra's house. He does not take Main Street. What is the shortest route he can take?
2. Chen walks to school every morning. He goes by the library, the museum, and the grocery store. How does he get to school?
3. Mandy likes to go to the library after school. She leaves school from the east exit and heads south. From the library she passes by the side of the museum. Show her route from school to home.
4. Diego walks to Zack's house on Saturday mornings. If he passes the museum, the library, the playground, the school, and the grocery store, how does he walk?
5. Two friends went to Mandy's house to play. One passed the park on the way home. The other passed the museum and the library. Who were the two friends?
6. The owner of the grocery store will sometimes deliver fresh produce to his customers. One day he delivered apples to the houses of Diego, Chen, Mandy, and Zack. Show the routes he could have taken and describe the order of his deliveries.
7. Show how Mandy can walk to Chen's house without passing by the museum.

Solutions to Map Two Problems*
1. Zack walks east on Third to American. He walks north on American to Fifth. He walks west on Fifth to Tyra's house.
2. Chen walks north on Main Street to Third. He walks east on Third to school.
3. Mandy walks south on American to First. She walks west on First to the library. From the library she walks west on first to Main Street. She walks north on Main Street to Second. She walks west on Second to get home.
4. Diego walks east on First to American. He walks north on American to Third. He walks west on Third to Zack's house.
5. The friend who passed the park is Tyra. The friend who passed the museum and the library is Chen.
6. One route would have taken him west on Third to Zack's house, south on Main Street to Chen's house, west on First to Diego's house, and north on Lake Drive to Mandy's house.
7. Mandy can walk east on Second to Hill, walk south—(southeast is one word) east on Hill to First, walk west on First to Main Street, and walk south on Main Street to Chen's house.

* In many cases, there are multiple answers that can be justified. If students are able to clearly explain their thinking, accept these alternate answers.

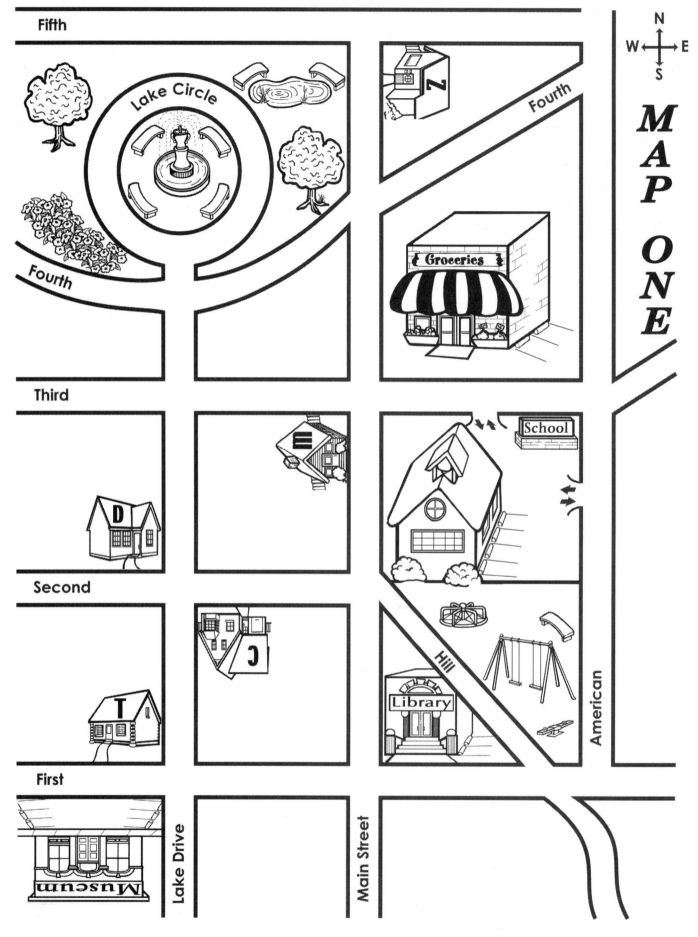

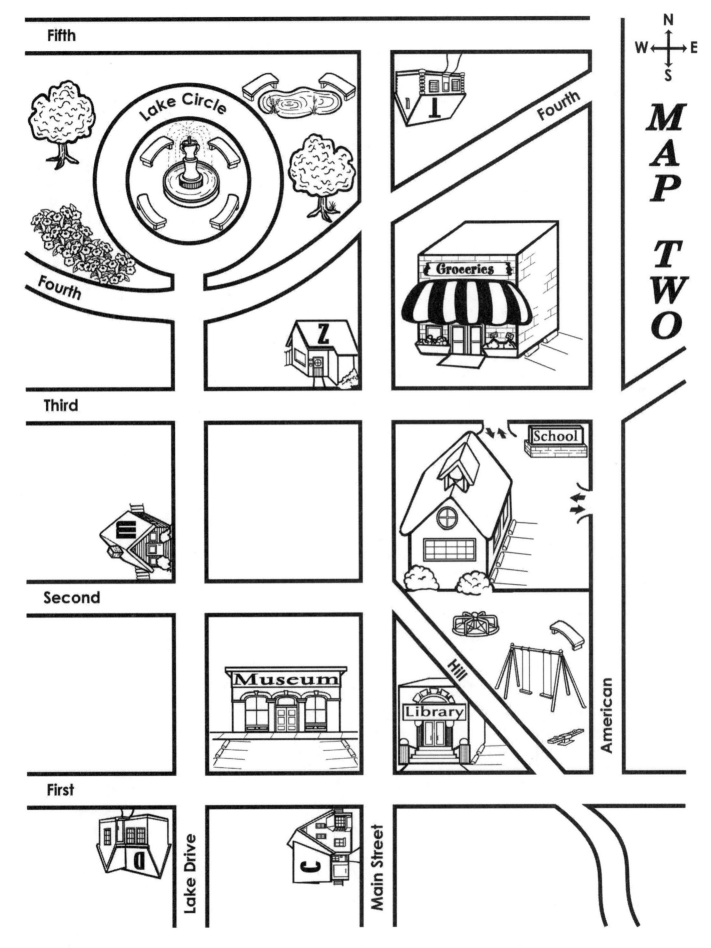

Problem-Solving Strategies
Wish for an Easier Problem

Sometimes a problem has so much data that it can be overwhelming. When this is the case, students can "wish for an easier problem," or simplify the problem by reorganizing the information. As they focus on how to solve the problem, rather than on the numbers and data involved, the problem becomes less complex and more manageable. This strategy is often used in conjunction with other strategies.

Tile Tallies

Topic
Problem solving

Key Question
How can you arrange Area Tiles so that it will be easy to count large numbers of them quickly?

Learning Goals
Students will:
1. work in groups to develop a way to make counting a large number of Area Tiles easier, and
2. evaluate the methods that are developed.

Guiding Document
NCTM Standards 2000*
- *Count with understanding and recognize "how many" in sets of objects*
- *Apply and adapt a variety of appropriate strategies to solve problems*
- *Build new mathematical knowledge through problem solving*
- *Monitor and reflect on the process of mathematical problem solving*

Math
Number sense
   counting
Problem solving

Integrated Processes
Observing
Organizing
Analyzing

Problem-Solving Strategies
Wish for an easier problem
Use manipulatives
Organize the information

Materials
Area Tiles (see *Management 2*)
9" x 12" construction paper, two pieces per group

Background Information
One problem-solving strategy that is useful in the primary grades is *wish for an easier problem*. Problems that seem daunting at first glance can be easily solved if they are first made simpler. When equipped with this strategy, young children can tackle problems that seem beyond their years and gain confidence in their abilities.

For adults and children alike, looking at a random arrangement of objects for five seconds and trying to count how many there are is a nearly impossible task. However, if this problem is made easier by organizing the objects in some fashion, the counting process becomes much simpler. This activity gives students the opportunity to find the most effective way to organize large numbers of Area Tiles so that they can be counted quickly.

Management
1. Each group will need a large number of Area Tiles. Each group should have a different amount. Determine what a "large number" is based on the ages and ability levels of your students.
2. Area Tiles can be purchased from AIMS in packages of 100 (#4810), 500 (#4811), and 1000 (# 4812). If you do not have Area Tiles, any other small, flat, uniform manipulative will work.

Procedure
1. Put 15-25 Area Tiles on the overhead projector with the projector off. Scatter them so that they are not organized in any way.
2. Tell students that you are going to see how good their counting skills are. Explain that you will turn on the overhead for five seconds and that they are to count all of the objects they see.
3. Turn on the overhead for five seconds. At the end of five seconds, turn it off, and ask students to write down how many tiles there were on the projector. (Hopefully they will complain that they weren't able to count them all, that there were too many, that they needed to see them for longer, etc.)
4. Tell students that they are going to have the opportunity to make this problem easier for their classmates. Explain that their challenge is to arrange a large set of tiles (like the one on the overhead) in such a way that another group can count all of them in only five seconds.
5. Have students get into groups and give each group a large number of Area Tiles and two pieces of construction paper. Be sure that no two groups have the same number of tiles.
6. Inform groups that they are to arrange the tiles on one of the pieces of construction paper. Once they are satisfied that they have an arrangement that will be easy to count, they should cover the arrangement with the second piece of construction paper.

7. After all groups have completed their arrangements, pair the groups up. Have the students from one group gather around the other group's table. Instruct one student to remove the top piece of construction paper and give the students five seconds to count the Area Tiles. Announce when the five seconds are up, and have the students replace the top piece of construction paper.
8. Allow the groups that were counting to discuss among themselves how many Area Tiles there were. Have them arrive at a group response and then compare that to the actual number of Area Tiles.
9. Have the groups switch roles and repeat this process.
10. Once all groups have had a chance to guess, discuss the methods used to arrange the Area Tiles. Based on which groups were able to correctly count the number of Area Tiles, determine the most effective method(s) of organization.
11. Arrange the tiles on the overhead projector using one of the most effective methods discovered by the students. Turn on the projector for another five seconds and give students the chance to count the tiles.
12. Compare this final experience to the initial experience and discuss what was better about this second one.

Connecting Learning
1. Were you able to count the tiles that were on the overhead the first time? Why or why not?
2. How did your group decide to arrange your tiles?
3. Was the other group able to count your tiles correctly in five seconds?
4. How did your group's method of arranging tiles compare to the methods of other groups?
5. Which ways of arranging tiles were the best? Why?
6. How else could you have made it easier to count all of the tiles in five seconds?
7. Were you able to count the tiles that were on the overhead the second time? Why or why not?

Extensions
1. Repeat this experience using tally marks or circles. (The tally marks can be arranged in groups of five, and the circles can be arranged like numbers on a die.)
2. Increase the number of tiles to make the problem more challenging.

* Reprinted with permission from *Principles and Standards for School Mathematics*, 2000 by the National Council of Teachers of Mathematics. All rights reserved.

Alphabet Soup

Topic
Problem solving

Key Question
How can you arrange letter cards so that you can look at them for five seconds and remember which letters you have?

Learning Goals
Students will:
1. work in groups to develop a way to make random letters easier to remember, and
2. determine the best method developed.

Guiding Document
NCTM Standards 2000*
- *Apply and adapt a variety of appropriate strategies to solve problems*
- *Solve problems that arise in mathematics and in other contexts*
- *Build new mathematical knowledge through problem solving*
- *Monitor and reflect on the process of mathematical problem solving*

Math
Number sense
   counting
Problem solving

Integrated Processes
Observing
Organizing
Analyzing

Problem-Solving Strategies
Wish for an easier problem
Use manipulatives
Organize the information

Materials
Letter cards (see *Management 2*)
9" x 12" construction paper, two pieces per group

Background Information
This activity is similar to *Tile Tallies,* but instead of looking at arrangements of tiles, students are challenged to remember a group of seemingly random letters. This task is difficult until the letters are made into words, allowing them to be easily remembered when viewed for a short period of time. This experience will reinforce techniques for making problems simpler in order to arrive at a solution.

Management
1. Each group will need a set of cards. Blank letter cards are provided for you to fill in. Suggested letter sets are provided at three levels—six-letter sets that form two three-letter words, seven-letter sets that form one three-letter word, and one four-letter word, and eight-letter sets that form two four-letter words. Select the letter set(s) that are most appropriate for your students, or make up your own.
2. It is recommended that students do the activity *Tile Tallies* before this experience.

Procedure
1. Write a set of letters (that will form words when rearranged) on the overhead projector. (See *Suggested Letter Sets.*) Do not make them into words or have them organized in any way.
2. Tell students that you are going to see how good their memories are. Explain that you will turn on the overhead for five seconds and that they are to try and remember all of the letters they see.
3. Turn on the overhead for five seconds. At the end of five seconds, turn it off and ask students to write down all the letters they can remember. (Hopefully they will complain that they weren't able to remember them all, that there were too many, that they needed to see them for a longer period of time, etc.)
4. Tell students that they are going to have the opportunity to make this problem easier for their classmates. Explain that their challenge is to arrange set of letters (like the one on the overhead) in such a way that another group can remember all of them after seeing them for only five seconds.
5. Have students get into groups and give each group a set of letter cards and two pieces of construction paper. Be sure that no two groups have the exact same letters.
6. Inform groups that they are to arrange the letter cards on one of the pieces of construction paper.

Once they are satisfied that they have an arrangement that will be easy to remember, they should cover the arrangement with the second piece of construction paper.

7. After all groups have completed their arrangements, pair the groups up. Have the students from one group gather around the other group's table. Instruct one student to remove the top piece of construction paper, and give the students five seconds to look at the letters. Announce when the five seconds are up, and have the students replace the top piece of construction paper.

8. Allow the groups that were looking at the letters to discuss among themselves what the letters were. Have them arrive at a group response and then compare that to the actual letters.

9. Have the groups switch roles and repeat this process.

10. Once all groups have had a chance to guess, discuss as a class the methods used to arrange the letter cards. Based on which groups were able to correctly remember all of the letters, determine the most effective method(s) of organization.

11. Rearrange the letters on the overhead so that they form words. Turn on the projector for another five seconds and give students the chance to look at the letters and try to remember them.

12. Compare this final experience to the initial experience and discuss what was better about this second one.

Connecting Learning

1. Were you able to remember all of the letters that were on the overhead the first time? Why or why not?
2. How did your group decide to arrange your letter cards?
3. Was the other group able to remember all of the letters you had after looking for five seconds?
4. How did your group's method of arranging letters compare to the methods of other groups?
5. Which ways of arranging letters were the best? Why? [Hopefully students in at least one group will have discovered that they can make words using their letters. If not, lead the class into a discovery of this method.]
6. How else could you have made it easier to remember all of the letters after looking for only five seconds?
7. Were you able to remember all of the letters that were on the overhead the second time? Why or why not?

Extensions

1. Have students play with the letter cards they have to see how many different words they can make using those letters.
2. Allow students to come up with their own sets of letter cards and trade these with classmates.
3. Increase the number of letter cards to make the problem more challenging.

Suggested Letter Sets

Level One—Two three-letter words
RED DOG
HER HAT
SEE SAW
HOW NOW
WHO TWO
ONE CAN
SAD CAT
BAD DOG

Level Two—One three-letter words and one four-letter word
BLUE BOY
BOOK BAG
HIS SHOE
RAT TRAP
RUN RAIN
FAR NEAR
NEW GAME
TEN CATS

Level Three—Two four-letter words
READ BOOK
BLUE BALL
RACE CARS
PLAY GAME
FOUR PENS
FIVE CANS
NINE TOYS
GIRL HAIR

* Reprinted with permission from *Principles and Standards for School Mathematics*, 2000 by the National Council of Teachers of Mathematics. All rights reserved.

Two-Colored Trains

Topic
Problem solving

Key Question
How many different trains can you make using five Unifix cubes in two colors?

Learning Goals
Students will:
1. determine how many different Unifix cube trains can be made using two, three, and four cubes in two colors;
2. look for patterns in their solutions; and
3. use what they have learned to determine how many five-cube trains are possible.

Guiding Document
NCTM Standards 2000*
- Apply and adapt a variety of appropriate strategies to solve problems
- Build new mathematical knowledge through problem solving
- Sort, classify, and order objects by size, number, and other properties

Math
Problem solving

Integrated Processes
Observing
Collecting and recording data
Organizing data
Applying

Problem-Solving Strategies
Wish for an easier problem
Look for patterns
Use manipulatives

Materials
Unifix cubes in two colors (see *Management 1*)
Crayons in colors to match the Unifix cubes
Student pages

Background Information
When problems seem overwhelming, it can help to start with a simpler problem. This can lead to the discovery of patterns or other insight that will help in solving the original challenge.

For a primary student, the question of how many different two-color trains you can make with five Unifix cubes is a difficult challenge. However, if students are first allowed to work on easier versions of the problem, they will be able to solve the more difficult problem as well.

Management
1. Students should work together in small groups of no more than four students.
2. Each group will need about 20 Unifix cubes of one color and 20 cubes of another color. (Colors need not be the same from group to group.)
3. When students are making their Unifix cube trains, it is important that they keep all the cubes of the same color together.

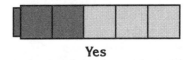
Yes

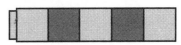
No

Emphasize that what is important is the number of each color used, not the arrangement of the colors within the train. For example, both the trains shown here are the same, because each uses three cubes of the lighter color and one cube of the darker color.

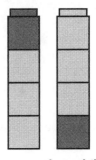

4. It is important to note that while the title of the activity is "Two-Colored Trains," trains that use only one of the two colors are included. Be sure to explain to students that they are to make all of the trains they can using the Unifix cubes they are given, even if some of those trains don't have both colors.

SOLVE IT! 2nd 164 © 2005 AIMS Education Foundation

Procedure

1. Ask students how many different Unifix cube trains they think they can make if they have two colors and each train has to be five cubes long.
2. Distribute the first two student pages and allow them to write their predictions.
3. Ask students what ideas they have for how they could solve the problem. Suggest that one way might be to try solving easier problems first.
4. Have students get in groups and distribute the two colors of Unifix cubes to each group. Ask the groups to show you every way that you can make a train of two Unifix cubes using those two colors. Tell students that not every train has to have both colors. (Hopefully students will be able to come up with three different solutions—two cubes of color A, two cubes of color B, and one cube each of colors A and B.)
5. Have students record their solutions on the student page by coloring in the trains to match the ones that they made.
6. Ask students to predict how many solutions there will be for three-cube trains. Tell students the rules for keeping cubes of the same color together in each train (see *Management 4*).
7. Have them work in groups to find and record all of the different three-cube solutions (three of color A, three of color B, two of color A and one of color B, two of color B and one of color A).
8. Repeat this process for four-cube trains.
9. Ask the groups how many four-cube trains they were able to find. If there are discrepancies among the groups, see if you can discover where the differences exist.
10. Invite students to try and organize their four-cube trains so that they can see some sort of pattern. If students have been consistent about how they have arranged their colors, they should be able to come up with something like this:

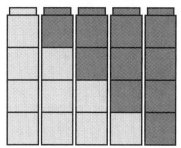

11. Tell students that they are now ready to try the original problem. Encourage students to revise their initial prediction about the number of five-cube trains based on what they have learned by doing the easier problems.
12. Have the groups find all of the five-cube trains. Record all of the solutions as a class, or allow students to record them on their student pages.
13. Close with a time of sharing in which students explain how they arrived at their solutions.

Connecting Learning

1. What did you learn by starting with an easier problem?
2. How did what you learned help you solve the harder problem?
3. Did you see any patterns in the Unifix cube trains? Explain.
4. How did these patterns help you solve the problem?
5. How many different trains can you make using six cubes and two colors?

Extensions

1. For students who are ready for an extra challenge, extend the problem to 10-cube trains. It takes 110 Unifix cubes—55 of one color and 55 of another color—to make all of the possible 10-cube trains; however, students should be given more cubes than that so that it is not obvious when they have gotten all of the solutions. A recording page has been included for this extension.
2. Try the problem with three colors of Unifix cubes.

* Reprinted with permission from *Principles and Standards for School Mathematics*, 2000 by the National Council of Teachers of Mathematics. All rights reserved.

Two-Colored Trains

How many 5-cube trains can you make with two colors of Unifix cubes?

I think there will be _____ different 5-cube trains.

Let's start with an easier problem!

How many 2-cube trains can you make?

I think I can make _____ 2-cube trains.

I made _____ 2-cube trains.

My 2-cube trains look like this:

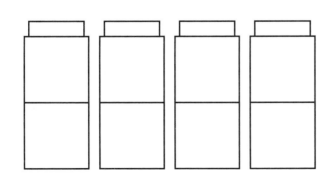

SOLVE IT! 2nd   166   © 2005 AIMS Education Foundation

Two-Colored Trains

How many 3-cube trains can you make?

I think I can make _____ 3-cube trains.

I made _____ 3-cube trains.

My 3-cube trains look like this:

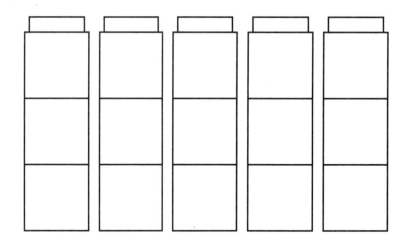

Two-Colored Trains

How many 4-cube trains can you make?

I think I can make _____ 4-cube trains.

I made _____ 4-cube trains.

My 4-cube trains look like this:

Two-Colored Trains

Now you are ready to solve our first question. How many 5-cube trains can you make?

Now I think I can make _____ 5-cube trains.

I made _____ 5-cube trains.

My 5-cube trains look like this:

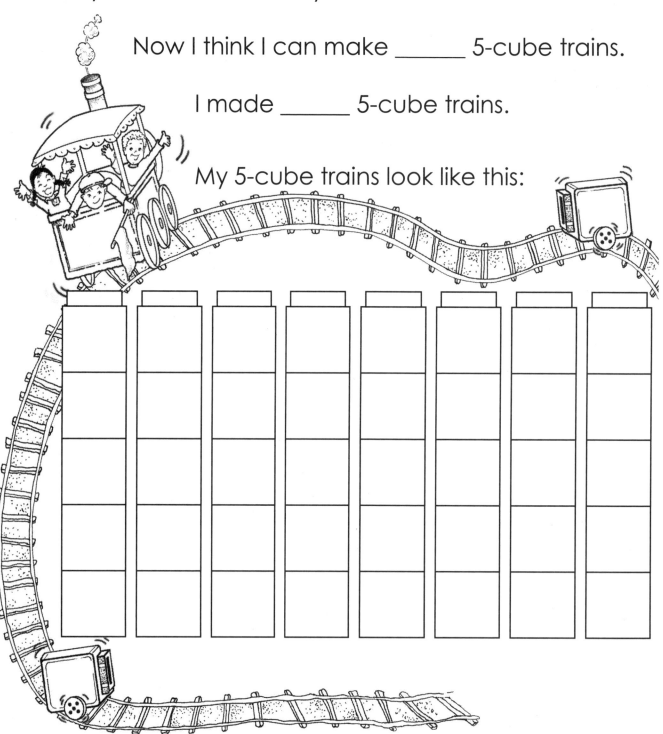

Two-Colored Trains

Extension

How many 10-cube trains can you make?

I think I can make _____ 10-cube trains.

I made _____ 10-cube trains.

My 10-cube trains look like this:

Practice Problems

The problems on the following pages are provided for additional practice with the problem-solving strategies covered in this book. No strategies have been recommended for the individual problems, and they do not follow any particular order. Students must decide which strategy to use based on the individual problem. It is suggested that the problems be copied onto transparencies and cut apart. A problem can then be placed on the overhead as a "bright beginning" to start math class or at any time during the day when a few minutes are available for review. To receive maximum benefit from the problems, be sure to have a time of discussion after each one where the emphasis is on the process and strategies used rather than arriving at the correct answer.

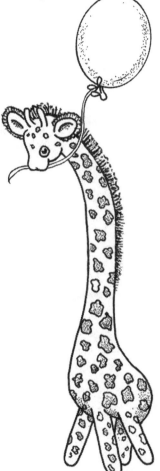

Tameka is 7 years old. Amy is 2 years older than Tameka. Nick is 3 years older than Amy. How old are Amy and Nick?	Diego is at the zoo. He sees 14 wings. How many storks? He sees 4 elephants. How many legs?
There were 2 ducks at the pond. Before long, 3 ducks came and 2 left. How many are left?	If you set the table for 4 people how many forks, spoons, and knives do you need altogether?
You have 8 wheels. How many scooters and race cars can you make? Will you have to make more of one than another?	Rob has 10 toy cars. He gets 2 new toy cars each week. How many toy cars does he have after 6 weeks?
The pattern is: A B A B A B … What is the 10th letter in the pattern?	What comes next? 18, 14, 10, 6, _____

What comes next? A, D, G, J, _____	I gave 3 marbles to a friend. I lost 5 on the way home. I have 6 marbles left. How many did I start with?
Draw a map from your classroom to the office.	Juan gave 2 bananas to his friend Kae. He gave 3 to his mother. He has 5 bananas left. How many bananas did Juan start with?
Do more people in your class buy or bring their lunch to school? Survey your classmates and graph the information.	Find all of the things in your desk that you can write with. Sort them and make a graph that tells me about them.
How does your class get to school? Survey your classmates and graph the data.	There are 6 animals in the farmyard. There are 18 legs total. How many are pigs and how many are ducks?

How many capital letters have both straight and curved lines?

Mai bought a candy bar. She paid with a dollar. She got $.45 in change. How much was the candy bar?

What comes next?

It takes 10 minutes to walk to school. School starts at 8:00. When do you need to leave home to arrive on time?

At school you start with an hour of math. Next is 30 minutes of reading. Then you have recess for 20 minutes. School starts at 8:30. What time does recess end?

I have a glass, a mug, and a pitcher. One has lemonade, one has milk, and one has water.
- The mug does not have water or milk.
- There is no water in the glass.

Which liquid is in which container?

I have to take my pets to the vet. I have 2 pet carriers. Each carrier can only hold 15 pounds. My pets weigh 8, 7, 6, 4, 3, and 2 pounds. What is one way to put my pets in the carriers?	Take four Unifix cubes: black, brown, white, and red. Build a tower using these clues: • The red is above the white. • The black is below the brown. • The white and brown are in the middle.
Help the coach line up the team from shortest to tallest. The players are Jerome, Rudy, Michael, Tony, and Kaden. • Jerome is taller than Rudy, but shorter than Tony. • Michael is shorter than Rudy, but taller than Kaden.	Mrs. Campbell, Mr. Lee, Miss Vang, and Mrs. Sanchez all have rooms on the first grade hall. • Mrs. Sanchez is in the third room on the hall. • Miss Vang's room is not first. • Mr. Lee's room is the last one on the hall. What is the order of the rooms?

Chen and Nori went fishing. They caught 17 fish total. Chen caught 3 fish more than Nori. How many fish did Chen catch? How many fish did Nori catch?

Jerome has some balloons. There are 7 pink balloons. There are 3 fewer blue balloons than pink balloons. There are 2 more red balloons than blue balloons. How many balloons are there?

Two friends surveyed their classmates. Here is what they found:

Favorite Ice Cream Survey Results

| Vanilla | Lorena Jerome Cassidy | Vanilla | IIII |
| Chocolate | Denzel Morgan Diego Haylie | Chocolate | ℍℕ I |

Which ice cream is more popular? How many people like chocolate better? How many people like vanilla better?

Kim was playing with some shapes. He put down a triangle, a square, and then a circle. How many circles would he need to repeat this pattern 5 times?

There were 15 cookies on 2 plates. When 3 cookies were taken away from the first plate, there were 7 cookies left on it. How many cookies were on the second plate?

There are 5 children out on the playground. The teacher called the children in for snack. She had 20 crackers. How many crackers did each child get?

The width of the rug in Mark's room is equal to 2 of his dad's feet or to 3 of his feet. If the length of the rug is equal to 4 of Dad's feet, then how many of Mark's feet is that?

Ms. Howard lives 60 miles from work. Her car goes 20 miles on one gallon of gas. How many gallons of gas does she need each day to go to and from work?

The AIMS Program

AIMS is the acronym for "**A**ctivities **I**ntegrating **M**athematics and **S**cience." Such integration enriches learning and makes it meaningful and holistic. AIMS began as a project of Fresno Pacific University to integrate the study of mathematics and science in grades K-9, but has since expanded to include language arts, social studies, and other disciplines.

AIMS is a continuing program of the non-profit AIMS Education Foundation. It had its inception in a National Science Foundation funded program whose purpose was to explore the effectiveness of integrating mathematics and science. The project directors in cooperation with 80 elementary classroom teachers devoted two years to a thorough field-testing of the results and implications of integration.

The approach met with such positive results that the decision was made to launch a program to create instructional materials incorporating this concept. Despite the fact that thoughtful educators have long recommended an integrative approach, very little appropriate material was available in 1981 when the project began. A series of writing projects have ensued, and today the AIMS Education Foundation is committed to continue the creation of new integrated activities on a permanent basis.

The AIMS program is funded through the sale of books, products, and staff development workshops and through proceeds from the Foundation's endowment. All net income from program and products flows into a trust fund administered by the AIMS Education Foundation. Use of these funds is restricted to support of research, development, and publication of new materials. Writers donate all their rights to the Foundation to support its on-going program. No royalties are paid to the writers.

The rationale for integration lies in the fact that science, mathematics, language arts, social studies, etc., are integrally interwoven in the real world from which it follows that they should be similarly treated in the classroom where we are preparing students to live in that world. Teachers who use the AIMS program give enthusiastic endorsement to the effectiveness of this approach.

Science encompasses the art of questioning, investigating, hypothesizing, discovering, and communicating. Mathematics is the language that provides clarity, objectivity, and understanding. The language arts provide us powerful tools of communication. Many of the major contemporary societal issues stem from advancements in science and must be studied in the context of the social sciences. Therefore, it is timely that all of us take seriously a more holistic mode of educating our students. This goal motivates all who are associated with the AIMS Program. We invite you to join us in this effort.

Meaningful integration of knowledge is a major recommendation coming from the nation's professional science and mathematics associations. The American Association for the Advancement of Science in *Science for All Americans* strongly recommends the integration of mathematics, science, and technology. The National Council of Teachers of Mathematics places strong emphasis on applications of mathematics such as are found in science investigations. AIMS is fully aligned with these recommendations.

Extensive field testing of AIMS investigations confirms these beneficial results:
1. Mathematics becomes more meaningful, hence more useful, when it is applied to situations that interest students.
2. The extent to which science is studied and understood is increased, with a significant economy of time, when mathematics and science are integrated.
3. There is improved quality of learning and retention, supporting the thesis that learning which is meaningful and relevant is more effective.
4. Motivation and involvement are increased dramatically as students investigate real-world situations and participate actively in the process.

We invite you to become part of this classroom teacher movement by using an integrated approach to learning and sharing any suggestions you may have. The AIMS Program welcomes you!

AIMS Education Foundation Programs

Practical proven strategies to improve student achievement

When you host an AIMS workshop for elementary and middle school educators, you will know your teachers are receiving effective usable training they can apply in their classrooms immediately.

Designed for teachers—AIMS Workshops:
- Correlate to your state standards;
- Address key topic areas, including math content, science content, problem solving, and process skills;
- Teach you how to use AIMS' effective hands-on approach;
- Provide practice of activity-based teaching;
- Address classroom management issues, higher-order thinking skills, and materials;
- Give you AIMS resources; and
- Offer college (graduate-level) credits for many courses.

Aligned to district and administrator needs—AIMS workshops offer:
- Flexible scheduling and grade span options;
- Custom (one-, two-, or three-day) workshops to meet specific schedule, topic and grade-span needs;
- Pre-packaged one-day workshops on most major topics—only $3,900 for up to 30 participants (includes all materials and expenses);
- Prepackaged *week-long* workshops (four- or five-day formats) for in-depth math and science training—only $12,300 for up to 30 participants (includes all materials and expenses);
- Sustained staff development, by scheduling workshops throughout the school year and including follow-up and assessment;
- Eligibility for funding under the Eisenhower Act and No Child Left Behind; and
- Affordable professional development—save when you schedule consecutive-day workshops.

University Credit—Correspondence Courses

AIMS offers correspondence courses through a partnership with Fresno Pacific University.
- Convenient distance-learning courses—you study at your own pace and schedule. No computer or Internet access required!

The tuition for each three-semester unit graduate-level course is $264 plus a materials fee.

The AIMS Instructional Leadership Program

This is an AIMS staff-development program seeking to prepare facilitators for leadership roles in science/math education in their home districts or regions. Upon successful completion of the program, trained facilitators become members of the AIMS Instructional Leadership Network, qualified to conduct AIMS workshops, teach AIMS in-service courses for college credit, and serve as AIMS consultants. Intensive training is provided in mathematics, science, process and thinking skills, workshop management, and other relevant topics.

Introducing AIMS Science Core Curriculum

Developed in alignment with your state standards, AIMS' Science Core Curriculum gives students the opportunity to build content knowledge, thinking skills, and fundamental science processes.
- *Each* grade specific module has been developed to extend the AIMS approach to full-year science programs.
- *Each* standards-based module includes math, reading, hands-on investigations, and assessments.

Like all AIMS resources these core modules are able to serve students at all stages of readiness, making these a great value across the grades served in your school.

For current information regarding the programs described above, please complete the following:

Information Request

Please send current information on the items checked:

____ *Basic Information Packet* on AIMS materials   ____ Hosting information for AIMS workshops
____ *AIMS Instructional Leadership Program*   ____ AIMS Science Core Curriculum

Name _____ Phone _____

Address _____
           Street   City   State   Zip

AIMS Magazine
YOUR K-9 MATH AND SCIENCE CLASSROOM ACTIVITIES RESOURCE

The AIMS Magazine is your source for standards-based, hands-on math and science investigations. Each issue is filled with teacher-friendly, ready-to-use activities that engage students in meaningful learning.

- *Four issues each year (fall, winter, spring, and summer).*

Current issue is shipped with all past issues within that volume.

| 1820 | Volume XX | 2005-2006 | $19.95 |
| 1821 | Volume XXI | 2006-2007 | $19.95 |

Two-Volume Combination

| M20507 | Volumes XX & XXI | 2005-2007 | $34.95 |

Back Volumes Available
Complete volumes available for purchase:

1802	Volume II	1987-1988	$19.95
1804	Volume IV	1989-1990	$19.95
1805	Volume V	1990-1991	$19.95
1807	Volume VII	1992-1993	$19.95
1808	Volume VIII	1993-1994	$19.95
1809	Volume IX	1994-1995	$19.95
1810	Volume X	1995-1996	$19.95
1811	Volume XI	1996-1997	$19.95
1812	Volume XII	1997-1998	$19.95
1813	Volume XIII	1998-1999	$19.95
1814	Volume XIV	1999-2000	$19.95
1815	Volume XV	2000-2001	$19.95
1816	Volume XVI	2001-2002	$19.95
1817	Volume XVII	2002-2003	$19.95
1818	Volume XVIII	2003-2004	$19.95
1819	Volume XIX	2004-2005	$35.00

Call today to order back volumes: 1.888.733.2467.

Call 1.888.733.2467 or go to www.aimsedu.org

Subscribe to the AIMS Magazine

$19.95 a year!

AIMS Magazine is published four times a year. Subscriptions ordered at any time will receive all the issues for that year.

AIMS Online – www.aimsedu.org

For the latest on AIMS publications, tips, information, and promotional offers, check out AIMS on the web at www.aimsedu.org. Explore our activities, database, discover featured activities, and get information on our college courses and workshops, too.

AIMS News

While visiting the AIMS website, sign up for AIMS News, our FREE e-mail newsletter. Published semi-monthly, AIMS News brings you food for thought and subscriber-only savings and specials. Each issue delivers:

- Thought-provoking articles on curriculum and pedagogy;
- Information about our newest books and products; and
- Sample activities.

Sign up today!

AIMS Program Publications

Actions with Fractions, 4-9
Awesome Addition and Super Subtraction, 2-3
Bats Incredible! 2-4
Brick Layers II, 4-9
Chemistry Matters, 4-7
Counting on Coins, K-2
Cycles of Knowing and Growing, 1-3
Crazy about Cotton, 3-7
Critters, 2-5
Down to Earth, 5-9
Electrical Connections, 4-9
Exploring Environments, K-6
Fabulous Fractions, 3-6
Fall into Math and Science, K-1
Field Detectives, 3-6
Finding Your Bearings, 4-9
Floaters and Sinkers, 5-9
From Head to Toe, 5-9
Fun with Foods, 5-9
Glide into Winter with Math & Science, K-1
Gravity Rules! 5-12
Hardhatting in a Geo-World, 3-5
It's About Time, K-2
It Must Be A Bird, Pre-K-2
Jaw Breakers and Heart Thumpers, 3-5
Looking at Geometry, 6-9
Looking at Lines, 6-9
Machine Shop, 5-9
Magnificent Microworld Adventures, 5-9
Marvelous Multiplication and Dazzling Division, 4-5
Math + Science, A Solution, 5-9
Mostly Magnets, 2-8
Movie Math Mania, 6-9
Multiplication the Algebra Way, 4-8
Off the Wall Science, 3-9
Our Wonderful World, 5-9
Out of This World, 4-8
Overhead and Underfoot, 3-5
Paper Square Geometry:
    The Mathematics of Origami, 5-12
Puzzle Play, 4-8
Pieces and Patterns, 5-9
Popping With Power, 3-5
Positive vs. Negative, 6-9

Primarily Bears, K-6
Primarily Earth, K-3
Primarily Physics, K-3
Primarily Plants, K-3
Problem Solving: Just for the Fun of It! 4-9
Proportional Reasoning, 6-9
Ray's Reflections, 4-8
Sense-Able Science, K-1
Soap Films and Bubbles, 4-9
Solve It! K-1: Problem-Solving Strategies, K-1
Solve It! 2nd: Problem-Solving Strategies, 2
Spatial Visualization, 4-9
Spills and Ripples, 5-12
Spring into Math and Science, K-1
The Amazing Circle, 4-9
The Budding Botanist, 3-6
The Sky's the Limit, 5-9
Through the Eyes of the Explorers, 5-9
Under Construction, K-2
Water Precious Water, 2-6
Weather Sense: Temperature, Air Pressure, and Wind, 4-5
Weather Sense: Moisture, 4-5
Winter Wonders, K-2

Spanish/English Editions*
Brinca de alegria hacia la Primavera con las
    Matemáticas y Ciencias, K-1
Cáete de gusto hacia el Otoño con las
    Matemáticas y Ciencias, K-1
Conexiones Eléctricas, 4-9
El Botanista Principiante, 3-6
Los Cinco Sentidos, K-1
Ositos Nada Más, K-6
Patine al Invierno con Matemáticas y Ciencias, K-1
Piezas y Diseños, 5-9
Primariamente Física, K-3
Primariamente Plantas, K-3
Principalmente Imanes, 2-8

* All Spanish/English Editions include student pages in Spanish and teacher and student pages in English.

Spanish Edition
Constructores II: Ingeniería Creativa Con Construcciones
    LEGO® 4-9
    The entire book is written in Spanish. English pages not included.

Other Science and Math Publications
Historical Connections in Mathematics, Vol. I, 5-9
Historical Connections in Mathematics, Vol. II, 5-9
Historical Connections in Mathematics, Vol. III, 5-9
Mathematicians are People, Too
Mathematicians are People, Too, Vol. II
What's Next, Volume 1, 4-12
What's Next, Volume 2, 4-12
What's Next, Volume 3, 4-12

For further information write to:
AIMS Education Foundation • P.O. Box 8120 • Fresno, California 93747-8120
www.aimsedu.org • Fax 559.255.6396

AIMS Duplication Rights Program

AIMS has received many requests from school districts for the purchase of unlimited duplication rights to AIMS materials. In response, the AIMS Education Foundation has formulated the program outlined below. There is a built-in flexibility which, we trust, will provide for those who use AIMS materials extensively to purchase such rights for either individual activities or entire books.

It is the goal of the AIMS Education Foundation to make its materials and programs available at reasonable cost. All income from the sale of publications and duplication rights is used to support AIMS programs; hence, strict adherence to regulations governing duplication is essential. Duplication of AIMS materials beyond limits set by copyright laws and those specified below is strictly forbidden.

Limited Duplication Rights

Any purchaser of an AIMS book may make up to *200 copies* of any activity in that book for use at *one school site*. Beyond that, rights must be purchased according to the appropriate category.

Unlimited Duplication Rights for Single Activities

An individual or school may purchase the right to make an unlimited number of copies of a single activity. The royalty is $5.00 per activity per school site.

Examples: 3 activities x 1 site x $5.00 = $15.00
              9 activities x 3 sites x $5.00 = $135.00

Unlimited Duplication Rights for Entire Books

A school or district may purchase the right to make an unlimited number of copies of a single, *specified* book. The royalty is $20.00 per book per school site. This is in addition to the cost of the book.

Examples: 5 books x 1 site   x $20.00 = $100.00
              12 books x 10 sites x $20.00 = $2400.00

Magazine Duplication Rights

Any purchaser of the *AIMS Magazine* is hereby granted permission to make up to 200 copies of any portion of it, provided these copies will be used for educational purposes.

Workshop Instructors' Duplication Rights

Workshop instructors may distribute to registered workshop participants a maximum of 100 copies of any article and/or 100 copies of no more than eight activities, provided these six conditions are met:

1. Since all AIMS activities are based upon the *AIMS Model of Mathematics* and the *AIMS Model of Learning*, leaders must include in their presentations an explanation of these two models.
2. Workshop instructors must relate the AIMS activities presented to these basic explanations of the AIMS philosophy of education.
3. The copyright notice must appear on all materials distributed.
4. Instructors must provide information enabling participants to apply for membership in the AIMS Education Foundation or order books from the Foundation.
5. Instructors must inform participants of their limited duplication rights as outlined below.
6. Only student pages may be duplicated.

Written permission must be obtained for duplication beyond the limits listed above. Additional royalty payments may be required.

Workshop Participants' Rights

Those enrolled in workshops in which AIMS student activity sheets are distributed may duplicate a maximum of 35 copies or enough to use the lessons one time with one class, whichever is less. Beyond that, rights must be purchased according to the appropriate category.

Application for Duplication Rights

The purchasing agency or individual must clearly specify the following:
1. Name, address, and telephone number
2. Titles of the books for Unlimited Duplication Rights contracts
3. Titles of activities for Unlimited Duplication Rights contracts
4. Names and addresses of school sites for which duplication rights are being purchased

NOTE: Books to be duplicated must be purchased separately and are not included in the contract for Unlimited Duplication Rights.

The requested duplication rights are automatically authorized when proper payment is received, although a *Certificate of Duplication Rights* will be issued when the application is processed.

Address all correspondence to: Contract Division
AIMS Education Foundation   www.aimsedu.org
P.O. Box 8120   Fax: 559.255.6396
Fresno, CA 93747-8120